Lifeline

BIOGRAPHIES

TUPAC SHAKUR
Hip-Hop Idol

by Carrie Golus

Twenty-First Century Books · Minneapolis

Twenty-First Century Books
A division of Lerner Publishing Group, Inc.
241 First Avenue North
Minneapolis, MN 55401 U.S.A.

Website address: www.lernerbooks.com

The publisher wishes to thank Phil Pruitt and Elena Keithley of USA TODAY for their help in preparing this book.

Library of Congress Cataloging-in-Publication Data

Golus, Carrie, 1969–
    Tupac Shakur: hip-hop idol / by Carrie Golus.
        p.   cm. — (USA Today lifeline biographies)
    Includes bibliographical references and index.
    ISBN 978–0–7613–5473–4 (lib. bdg. : alk. paper)
    1. Shakur, Tupac, 1971–1996—Juvenile literature. 2. Rap musicians—United States—Biography—Juvenile literature. I. Title.
ML3930.S48G65 2011
782.421649092—dc22 [B]   2009038127

Manufactured in the United States of America
1 – VI – 7/15/10

USA TODAY · Lifeline BIOGRAPHIES

USA TODAY

INTRODUCTION

2Pac: Best-selling rap artist Tupac Shakur was twenty-five years old when he was shot to death in 1996 while riding in a car in Las Vegas, Nevada.

"How Long Will They Mourn Me?"

Las Vegas, Nevada, was burning hot on Friday, September 13, 1996. Outside the University Medical Center, a small crowd sweated. The temperature soared to 100°F (38°C). The group was mostly young, mostly African American. There were dozens of children. They were there because of Tupac Shakur, the rapper as famous for his police record as for his music. Inside the hospital, Tupac was fighting for his life.

Friends in business: Tupac *(left)* had a recording contract with Death Row Records. Marion "Suge" Knight owned the record label. They are shown here in August 1996 in Los Angeles, California.

Six days before, Tupac had been shot four times. He had been riding in a car driven by Marion "Suge" Knight. Knight was a close friend. He also owned Death Row Records, Tupac's record label. At a stoplight, a white Cadillac pulled up next to Knight's car. Someone inside opened fire. Tupac was hit twice in the chest, once in the hand, and once in the leg. Knight wasn't seriously hurt.

Still, few people thought Tupac would die. He had already survived one shooting two years before. That time he took five bullets. Two of them were to the head. And yet he had checked himself out of the hospital the very same day. "I haven't seen anybody in my twenty-five-year... career leave the hospital like this," Dr. Leon Pachter, one of Tupac's surgeons, had told reporters afterward.

But the Las Vegas shooting was much more serious. Knight and Tupac's mother, Afeni, were at the hospital. Tupac couldn't get out of bed. On his third day, doctors took out his right lung. They also gave him drugs to put him into a coma (deep sleep). They did so to keep him from trying to get out of bed and hurting himself. On the seventh day, he gave up the fight. Tupac died at 4:03 P.M. He was twenty-five years old.

"If I Die 2night"

News of Tupac's death spread quickly. The crowd outside the hospital grew larger. Many of the mourners wept. Some stared blankly into space. Others spilled liquor on the ground in Tupac's honor. A long line of cars circled the area. Many of them blasted Tupac's music. The most popular songs were those about death, such as "If I Die 2night."Afeni

Bullet damage: The black BMW Tupac and Marion Knight were in on September 7, 1996, sits in an impound lot a few days after the shooting.

Hospital visit: Marion Knight walks past the crowd into the Las Vegas hospital where Tupac was being treated after the fatal shooting.

Shakur left the hospital, surrounded by family. Knight showed no emotion as he pushed through the crowd. There was just one moment of anger. A friend of Tupac's screamed at the hospital staff. He demanded to know why they'd let Tupac die. Hundreds of police officers made sure the mourning stayed peaceful. But there was no violence. There was just a feeling of deep sadness. "I hope you tell the truth about Tupac," one young mourner told a reporter for *Rolling Stone*. "He was a hero to me, and he kept it real for the hood [neighborhood]."

The Rap About Tupac: Life of conflicting images comes to a violent end

<u>From the Pages of USA TODAY</u>

Stacy Bell wiped tears from her eyes as she stood before the makeshift shrine honoring slain rapper Tupac Shakur. "I've been upset all weekend," said Bell, who works at AMC Music and Video store in San Bernardino, Calif., and helped create the memorial of photos, hats and 2Pac CDs. "I feel like he had a lot to still offer to the younger people," said Bell, 25.

Whether the artist who overcame poverty to become one of gangsta rap's biggest stars really was changing will never be known. But his Friday-the-13th death from respiratory failure and cardiopulmonary arrest in Las Vegas six days after being shot is once again raising questions about the controversial music and its influence.

"Many fans are acting like he was some type of hero or some type of martyr," Tom Joyner, nationally syndicated radio host, said Sunday. "Fans should be asking themselves: 'What can we learn from this?' But many view him as a god. What does this say about our society?"

It says his music and life were as contradictory as the society it reflects. At the Brooklyn [New York] church Shakur attended as a teen, he was mourned Sunday as the victim of a society that destroys black youth. To others, he was written off as another violent rapper glorifying gangsta culture in his music—living by the lyrics, dying by the lyrics, getting what he deserved.

Shakur was riding with Death Row Records chief Marion "Suge" Knight Jr., 31, to a nightclub when he was shot four times. He was 25. Police say they have no suspects, no motive and no leads. No one from Death Row, including Knight, has commented on the case. The same goes for Interscope Records, distributor of Death Row, and MCA Music, the 50% owner of Interscope.

"Sometimes the lure of violent culture is so magnetic that even when one overcomes it with material success, it continues to call," Jesse Jackson, who prayed with Shakur's mother at the rapper's bedside last Sunday, told *The Los Angeles Times*. "He couldn't break the cycle."

—Edna Gundersen; Bruce Haring; Ann Oldenburg;
Contributing: Andre Montgomery

Son of a Panther

Tupac's mother was a leader in the Black Panthers, an African American political group of the 1960s. The Black Panthers worked to spread their message of "black power." Afeni and twenty other Panthers had been arrested on April 2, 1969. They were called the New York 21. The police said the group had planned to blow up several places in New York.

Tupac's mother: Afeni Shakur is shown here in 1971, when she was a member of the Black Panthers. The Black Panthers were a radical political group.

While out on bail (money posted to get out of jail until trial), Afeni became pregnant. She was not sure who the father was. It may have been Billy Garland, another Black Panther. Or it may have been a local drug dealer, Kenneth "Legs" Sanders. At the time, Afeni was living with Lumumba Shakur. Shakur was another member of the New York 21. When he found out she was pregnant by another man, he kicked her out.

Afeni Shakur was born Alice Faye Williams. She was named after Alice Faye, a singer and movie star of the 1930s and 1940s. Afeni changed her name after joining the Black Panthers in the 1960s.

IN FOCUS

The Black Panthers

The Black Panthers was a group founded by Huey Newton and Bobby Seale in Oakland, California, in 1966. Like Martin Luther King Jr., the Black Panthers fought for equality for African Americans. But they did not agree with King's nonviolent approach. When King and his followers were attacked during civil rights marches, they never fought back. But the Panthers believed in defending themselves.

The Black Panthers ran many useful programs. They gave free breakfast to poor children. They set up free health clinics in black neighborhoods. They also fought against police brutality. Sometimes, armed Black Panthers followed police officers around as they patrolled black neighborhoods.

Afeni Shakur began going to Black Panther meetings in 1968. She was twenty-two. Soon she became one of the few powerful women in the nearly all-male group. Afeni pushed for women to have an equal role in the party. For example, she wanted female Panthers to get weapons training just as the men did.

The Federal Bureau of Investigation (FBI) thought the Black Panthers were a threat. FBI agents joined the group to destroy it from within. Partly because of the FBI's efforts, the Black Panthers fell apart in the early 1970s.

Afeni helped raise bail for other members of the New York 21. But when two male members of the group left town, authorities sent her back to jail. Life at the New York Women's House of Detention was hard. Afeni had to get a court order so she could have one egg and a glass of milk every morning. She lost weight, but her baby kept growing. "I had never been able to carry a child past three months of pregnancy," Afeni said. "But in the midst of this, this child stayed."

Together, the members of the New York 21 were charged with 156 counts (crimes). They faced a combined 352 years in prison. Afeni served as her own lawyer, even though she had no education in law. Fearing the worst, she hoped her sister would raise her child. Instead, on May 13, 1971, Afeni and thirteen other members of the New York 21 were cleared of all charges.

 According to some sources, Tupac's name at first was Lesane Parish Crooks. Afeni changed his name shortly after his birth.

On June 16, 1971, Tupac Amaru Shakur was born in New York. Tupac Amaru means "shining serpent." This was the name of a warrior in Peru in the 1700s. Shakur means "thankful to God" in Arabic. To Afeni, Tupac's birth was a miracle. "I knew, my gut knew, something about this child: that he wasn't supposed to be here. And he was!" she said later. "And he was strong and he was . . . spirited and just the prettiest smile in the world. What a wonderful, wonderful spirit this child was right from the beginning."

IN F🔎CUS

Túpac Amaru II

Túpac Amaru II (1742–1781) was the last leader of the Incas. These people, native to Peru, were conquered by Spain in the 1500s. Born José Gabriel Condorcanqui, Amaru later named himself after his great-grandfather. In 1780 he and his followers tried to defeat the Spaniards. The attempt failed. Amaru and most of his family were killed. But he became a famous symbol in the struggle for freedom.

Artist in the making: Tupac began writing plays when he was six years old. His cousins would help him act out his plays.

A Young Talent

By the time Tupac was born, Billy Garland was out of Afeni's life. Legs, Tupac's other possible father, did not go away completely. Afeni named Geronimo and Linda Pratt as godparents. But for the most part, she had to raise her son alone. As a parent, Afeni did not believe in hiding the truth. "She just told me, 'I don't know who your daddy is,'" Tupac said. (Tupac later accepted that Garland was his father.)

Geronimo Pratt

Tupac's godfather was Geronimo Pratt. Pratt was a high-ranking member of the Black Panthers. He went to prison in 1972 for murder and kidnapping. He claimed he had been falsely accused. Pratt's lawyer, Johnnie Cochran, fought for more than twenty years to free him. Pratt finally was freed in 1997 after his trial was ruled to be unfair. Some think his sentence was part of the FBI's efforts to destroy the Black Panthers. Pratt could not be a real father figure to Tupac. He was in prison during Tupac's entire childhood. But he wrote Tupac many kind letters.

At first, Afeni did well on her own. After her trial, she was treated like a minor star. She gave talks at Yale University and Harvard University. Later, she took a job at Bronx Legal Services in New York City. Afeni worked there as an assistant.

In the mid-1970s, Afeni became involved with Mutulu Shakur. Mutulu was Lumumba Shakur's adopted brother. Mutulu had been a member of the Black Panthers and other activist groups. The couple did not marry. But Mutulu thought of himself as Tupac's stepfather. Afeni and Mutulu had a daughter, Tupac's half sister Sekyiwa (pronounced Seht-CHOO-wah). Mutulu also had several other children. Among them was Maurice Harding, who later became the rapper Mopreme.

Ten-Year-Old Revolutionary

Tupac showed creative talent early. He began writing plays when he was just six years old. He always wanted everything to be just perfect. He never let anyone else direct his plays. The actors (his cousins) had to follow his rules exactly. "He would have make-believe singing groups," Afeni said. "He would be Prince, or Ralph in New Edition. He was always the lead."

Tupac wrote poetry and love songs. He also kept a diary. "In that book I said I was going to be famous," he later said. He loved to read, a habit he picked up from his mother. When he was bad, Afeni sometimes punished him by making him read the entire *New York Times* newspaper.

Afeni joined the House of the Lord Church in Brooklyn when Tupac was ten. The pastor, Herbert Daughtry, once asked Tupac what he wanted to be when he grew up. He answered, "I want to be a revolutionary!" The Black Panthers was no longer an active group. But Tupac was still deeply moved by the views of his mother and the people she knew.

 Afeni took Tupac to his first political speech when he was just days old.

Around the same time, Mutulu was accused of working with others to commit armed robbery and murder. The FBI put Mutulu on its ten most wanted list. He had to leave the family to go into hiding.

IN FOCUS

Mutulu Shakur on Trial

The FBI captured Mutulu Shakur in 1986. Mutulu claimed he was a freedom fighter in the struggle for African American equality. He said the court had no right to try him. If a trial was needed, Mutulu said that he should be treated as a prisoner of war. Some experts agreed with him. But the judge rejected his idea. In 1988 Mutulu was sentenced to sixty years in prison.

May 12, 1988

7 radicals indicted in Capitol bombing

<u>From the Pages of</u>
<u>USA TODAY</u>

Seven radical leftists have been indicted [charged] in the bombing of the U.S. Capitol—an action the government said Wednesday signaled "the last gasp" of 1960s-70s revolutionary groups. Announcement of the indictments—sealed since April—came after one of the seven, Marilyn Jean Buck, was convicted in New York for 1981's bloody Brink's heists that left four lawmen dead. Her conviction—along with Mutulu Shakur—was the last for the Brink's robberies used to finance terror activities. "Let this be a warning to those who seek to influence the government through violence and terrorism," said U.S. Attorney Jay Stephens.

Indicted with Buck: Laura Whitehorn, Linda Evans, Susan Rosenberg, Elizabeth Duke, Timothy Blunk and Alan Berkman. All but Duke are in jail. The bombing Nov. 7, 1983, blew a hole in a wall outside the U.S. Senate and damaged five paintings. No one was hurt.

All seven had connections to members of radical groups such as the Weather Underground and Black Liberation Army, which staged the bloody 1981 Brink's robberies in the Bronx and in Rockland County, N.Y. The group got $1.6 million in the Rockland heist. The bloodshed drove the group underground. "What the indictments reflected were that these people had regressed to tactics being used by the Weather Underground," said John Castelucci, a reporter at the *Providence (R.I.) Journal* and author of *The Big Dance*, which chronicled the Rockland heist.

—Tim Doherty

Possibly because of her link to Mutulu, Afeni lost her job at Bronx Legal Services. Afeni had not been rich before. But now she had to struggle to support her two children.

Afeni and the children moved often between the Bronx and Harlem, another part of New York City. At the worst times, they were homeless. All the moving around hurt Tupac deeply. Other kids bullied him. "I remember crying all the time. My major thing growing up was I couldn't fit in," Tupac said years later. "Because I was from everywhere, I didn't have no buddies that I grew up with. Every time I had to go to a new apartment, I had to [start over]. People think just because you born in the ghetto you gonna fit in. A little twist in your life and you don't fit in no matter what."

Legs lived with the family in the early 1980s. He spent time with Tupac. They would go to the barbershop or out for hamburgers. But Legs wasn't really a good influence. He was the one who first gave Afeni crack. She quickly became addicted to this powerful new form of cocaine.

Tupac was hurt by the lack of a steady father figure. His mother taught him how to cook, sew, and take care of a house. But she could not teach him how to be a man. "It made me bitter seeing all these other [kids] with fathers gettin' answers to questions that I have," he said. "Even now I still don't get 'em."

On the move: Tupac and his mother and sister moved often when he was young. Sometimes they lived in Harlem, an African American neighborhood in New York City. A Harlem apartment building is shown here in 1970. Two boys play with a dog out front.

Musical history: The Apollo Theater is one of the best-known landmarks in the Harlem neighborhood of New York City. Many famous musicians have performed there.

Young Actor and Rapper
In 1983, when Tupac was twelve, Afeni signed him up with a theater group in Harlem. It was called the 127th Street Ensemble. The same year, Tupac made his first appearance onstage. He went onstage with the group at Harlem's famous Apollo Theater. He played Travis in the play *A Raisin in the Sun*. Tupac was the only child in the cast. At one point in the play, he was the only actor on the stage. Tupac loved the attention. But even more, he loved getting away from reality. "I didn't like my life, but through acting, I could become somebody else," he said.

 Tupac's performance in *A Raisin in the Sun* helped raise money for the 1984 presidential run of civil rights leader Jesse Jackson Sr.

Soon afterward, Legs went to prison for credit card fraud. Afeni and her children moved to White Plains, New York. There, they stayed

A Raisin in the Sun

Lorraine Hansberry

A Raisin in the Sun is a play by Lorraine Hansberry. She wrote it in 1959. It was the first play written by an African American woman to be staged on Broadway in New York. *A Raisin in the Sun* is about a working-class African American family that buys a home in a white neighborhood. The play follows the troubles the family members have as they try to adjust to a new home.

The play reflects events from Hansberry's life. When she was a child, her family moved into Woodlawn, a white neighborhood on the South Side of Chicago, Illinois. Hansberry remembered how unkind many of her neighbors were. Even as an adult, she felt very bitter about the experience.

in a hotel that was paid for by public aid. In 1985 they moved in with Afeni's cousin in Baltimore, Maryland. When the family was settled, Afeni tried to contact Legs. But she learned he had died after a heart attack from smoking crack. He was just forty-one years old. Tupac was angry about Legs's death. But he didn't cry about it for more than three months. "After he did," Afeni recalled, "he told me, 'I miss my daddy.'" Tupac went to Rolling Park Junior High until eighth grade. Then he earned a spot at the famous Baltimore School for the Arts (BSA). He was one of the high school's few African American students. "That was the first time I saw there was white people who you could get along with," Tupac said. "Before that, I just believed what everybody else said: they was devils." He had several white girlfriends at BSA. For the first time, Tupac felt as though he fit in.

He also felt supported by the teachers, most of whom were white. Donald Hickens was the head of the school's theater department. He saw Tupac as a talented, serious actor. Hickens tried to do what he could to help him succeed. "For Tupac it was a new experience to be around white people who really cared about him," Hickens said. Tupac enjoyed his classes. He read the plays of Shakespeare,

Making friends: Tupac *(upper left)* poses with some of his friends, including Jada Pinkett *(top right)* at the Baltimore School for the Arts.

took ballet, and went to Broadway shows. Even in a group of talented young people, Tupac stood out. "I loved going to school," he said. "It taught me a lot. I was starting to feel like I really wanted to be an artist." One of his closest friends at BSA was dance student Jada Pinkett. They shared a painful bond. Pinkett's mother also used crack. Pinkett was shocked by how poor Tupac's family was. He owned just two pairs of pants and two sweaters. He slept on a mattress with no sheets. Many times, the fridge was empty and the electricity was shut off.

First influence: When Tupac was a teenager, he listened to rap music by LL Cool J, shown here in 2000.

But Tupac had a small radio. In 1987, at the age of sixteen, he first heard "I'm Bad" by rapper LL Cool J. "I was writing rhymes by candle-light and I knew I was gonna be a rapper," he said. Tupac's first stage name was MC New York. He wrote his first rap after a friend was shot. The song was about gun control.

Tupac was doing well in Baltimore. But Afeni was not. She had an abusive boyfriend. She used crack often. In 1988, by the end of Tupac's junior year, Afeni could no longer cope with her problem. She sent

Tupac and his sister to live in Marin City, California. They moved in with Tupac's godmother, Linda Pratt. Tupac was sad that he had to quit BSA. "Leaving that school affected me so much," he said. "Even now, I see that as the point where I got off track."

USA TODAY Snapshots®

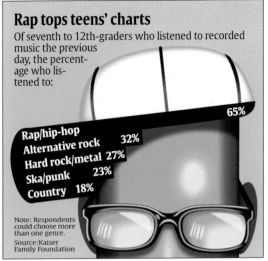

Rap tops teens' charts

Of seventh to 12th-graders who listened to recorded music the previous day, the percentage who listened to:

Rap/hip-hop 65%
Alternative rock 32%
Hard rock/metal 27%
Ska/punk 23%
Country 18%

Note: Respondents could choose more than one genre.

Source: Kaiser Family Foundation

By Rebecca Pollack and Bob Laird, USA TODAY, 2005

Marin County is one of the richest places in California. But Tupac's new hometown of Marin City was an island of poverty within the county. The people there didn't share the rest of the county's wealth. Fewer than three thousand people, mostly African American, lived in the town.

Marin County: Tupac's new home, Marin City, was in picturesque and affluent Marin County. People in Marin City, however, lived in poverty.

The Jungle

Tupac's new life in Marin City, nicknamed the Jungle, was hard. Once again, he was the new kid trying to fit in. "It was like a hood and I wanted to be a part of it," he said. What he found was kindness but no respect. "I got love but the kind of love you would give a dog or a neighborhood crack fiend. They liked me because I was at the bottom." Afeni had sent her children to live with Linda Pratt because Afeni wanted them to be safe. But Pratt was an alcoholic. Sometimes when she drank, she screamed at Tupac and Sekyiwa. When Pratt went into treatment for her alcohol problem, Afeni moved to California to look after her children. Life with Afeni was just as grim. Her crack use was out of control. Sometimes, she would disappear for months. She left her children to take care of themselves.

In the fall of 1988, Tupac began attending Tamalpais High School. Even though the school was in rich Marin County, Marin City itself was poor. Tupac had been a star at the Baltimore School for the Arts. But with his home life so unstable, he cut classes and let his schoolwork slide.

In his first videotaped interview, at the age of seventeen, Tupac spoke with a strong New York accent. His accent faded after a few years of living in California.

Tupac often stayed with friends rather than going home. Later, he moved in with a group of boys who lived in a vacant apartment. By this time, he was writing poetry and rap songs. His life was reflected in his lyrics. He recalled these dark days in the song "Dear Mama." According to the song, his mother kicked him out when he was just seventeen. Tupac and his mother had little contact. "In New York and all those times we was growing up, she was my hero," Tupac said. But when crack took over Afeni's life, he lost all respect for her.

At the age of eighteen, Tupac dropped out of high school. But he kept reading. It was his way to educate himself. He pursued music, writing, and rapping whenever he got the chance. He also listened to a wide range of music. He liked English and Irish pop. Among his favorite artists were Kate Bush, Culture Club, Sinead O'Connor, and U2. He once said that his favorite piece of music was the theme song from the Broadway musical *Les Misérables*.

December 21, 2007

More places turning to drug courts

From the Pages of
USA TODAY
Damon Fuseyamore vividly recalls smoking "my last nickel of crack" on June 16, 1997, while sitting on the steps outside his New York City residence. He had been arrested two weeks before "with six nickels of crack and a bunch of money." He was charged with selling crack and was looking at two to seven years in prison. But he had another option. "I had a choice of doing jail time or changing my life and going through treatment," he said. "Any smart person would take the program."

Fuseyamore, 45 and the father of a 10-year-old son, celebrated 10 years of sobriety in June, according to Dennis Reilly, former director of the Brooklyn Treatment Court. Fuseyamore's story is one of thousands touted by supporters of alternative drug courts.

The courts began 18 years ago as an experiment to attack a growing crack cocaine epidemic. They rely on treatment, rigorous supervision and accountability as a way to help, for the most part, non-violent drug users rather than sending them to prison. There are now 2,016 drug courts in about 1,100 counties, according to the National Drug Court Institute.

"We're scratching the surface. I think it's critical that a drug court is in every county in America," said [West] Huddleston [CEO of the institute], who estimates that 120,000 people are served annually by drug court alternatives.

—David Unze

Hip-Hop Dreams

The hip-hop scene in northern California was strong. It gave Tupac the chance to pursue his music. With new friend Ray Luv, Tupac formed a rap group called Strictly Dope. The two rapped at local clubs and house parties. They didn't make much money. But Tupac was writing and rapping. He was doing what he loved.

The recordings of Strictly Dope were released in 2001 under the name *Tupac Shakur: The Lost Tapes.*

To make money, Tupac sometimes sold crack. But his Marin City friends—many of them drug dealers themselves—told him to stop. They saw Tupac's talent. They didn't want him to get caught up in the drug life. "I had so many loans from dope dealers, and I've never been able to repay because they're not here anymore," Tupac said. "They would just say, 'Here. Make that album. Mention my name.'" Tupac wanted to break into the music industry. But he didn't know how. That changed in the spring of 1989. He had a chance meeting with Leila Steinberg. Steinberg, a young writer, teacher, and music producer, would become his first manager.

Steinberg was sitting in a Marin City park. She was reading a book written by Winnie Mandela. Winnie was the wife of anti-apartheid leader Nelson Mandela of South Africa. To Steinberg's surprise, Tupac

IN FOCUS

Nelson Mandela and Apartheid

Apartheid is the official policy of racial segregation in South Africa from 1948 to 1994. Nelson Mandela was a leader in the African National Congress, which fought apartheid. Because of his position, he was imprisoned for twenty-eight years, from 1962 to 1990. Four years after his release, Mandela became South Africa's first black president.

Nelson Mandela

walked up to her and began quoting lines from the book. The two started talking.

Steinberg invited Tupac to a weekly poetry group that met at her house. Group members wrote, read, and discussed poetry. Tupac impressed the group. "He was a genius who became the group's greatest inspiration," Steinberg said. When she found out Tupac was homeless, she offered to let him move in with her and her family.

First manager: Tupac met Leila Steinberg (*above*) at a city park in Marin City. He started attending weekly poetry group meetings at her house. Eventually, she became his manager.

Tupac's friendship with Steinberg was based on a love of books and learning. "We searched for knowledge," she said. "We explored

IN FOCUS

The Rose That Grew from Concrete

After Tupac's death, Leila Steinberg kept his notebooks. They included the poems he wrote for her poetry circle. These early poems were released in 2000 under the title *The Rose That Grew from Concrete*. The book includes copies of Tupac's original notebook pages. The poems are printed in his own handwriting.

together." Tupac went with Steinberg to local schools, where she taught her writing workshops. She taught, and he rapped. "At seventeen," Steinberg recalled, "he was wide-eyed, and really believed that he could change the world."

Soon after their first meeting, Steinberg introduced Tupac to Atron Gregory. Gregory had started his own record label, TNT. Among his recording artists was the successful Bay Area rap group Digital Underground. Digital Underground's song "The Humpty Dance" was one of the first hip-hop songs played in clubs. It also became a number eleven hit on the pop charts.

Steinberg helped Tupac get a tryout with Digital Underground's lead rapper, Gregory "Shock G" Jacobs. At first, Shock G noticed Tupac's professional manner. Then, once Tupac performed for him, he was impressed with his rapping. "It was street. It was educated," Shock G said.

Tupac's early lyrics were either political or "hip-hop fantasy," Shock G said. An example of the hip-hop fantasy was the song "The Case of the Misplaced Mic." In the song, Tupac has to go to a rap battle without his beloved microphone. At the end of the battle, Tupac's opponent is dead. Then he finds that his mic was in his pocket all along.

Music business: Tupac got his start in rap music with the Oakland-based group Digital Underground.

Digital Underground: Tupac *(left)* performs with Digital Underground in New Jersey in 1990.

In 1990 Tupac joined Digital Underground for their tour of the United States and Japan. He worked as a roadie. His job was to carry and set up equipment. He helped the band members in any way he could. He also danced onstage behind the main show. Tupac's duties included dancing with a life-size rubber doll during "The Humpty Dance."

Rebel of the Underground

Tupac was happy to be dancing with Digital Underground. But he wanted to do more. "Every chance he get, he'd get on the mic—after the shows, at the after-parties," Shock G said. "Once people saw him, that was history." Soon, Tupac earned the chance to do some background rapping (performing shorter parts to support the main rapper). He didn't like sharing the spotlight, though. Sometimes he would sing when he wasn't supposed to. Shock G would tell him to stop.

IN FOCUS

Digital Underground

Digital Underground was one of the first hit rap groups from the West Coast. The band was known for its fun, adult party music. Greg "Shock G" Jacobs was the lead rapper. He rapped in the band as himself and as Humpty Hump. Humpty Hump was a comic character who wore a fake nose and sang in a nasal style. During concerts, a silent stand-in would play either Shock G or Humpty Hump. Then after a noisy distraction, Shock G would switch roles. Digital Underground's biggest hit was "The Humpty Dance." The song made it to number eleven on the pop charts.

"The Humpty Dance": Digital Underground (*shown above*) had their biggest hit with "The Humpty Dance," in 1990. The group was constantly changing and getting new members.

Tupac would argue back. Shock G would kick him off the tour. Then the fight would blow over. Tupac would be back in the group as if nothing had happened.

Tupac's talent was obvious. But so was his temper. His new nickname was Rebel of the Underground. The name referred to his Panther background and his rebellious nature.

Tupac was small. He stood just five feet eight and weighed 150 pounds (68 kilograms). Even though he wasn't big, he didn't avoid fights. Once, while on tour, Tupac got angry with the soundman for making a mistake. Tupac was just about to punch the man. Gregory held Tupac back. "We were like, yo, Pac, you can't beat up the soundman!" said Ronald "Money-B" Brooks, Digital Underground's second rapper. "But he's crazy."

In 1991 Tupac had his first chance to rap on a record in the song "Same Song." As in much of Tupac's later work, the lyrics were about himself. He rapped about how girls didn't care about him before. But once he became famous, suddenly they did. Tupac's part in "Same

IN FOCUS

Underground Railroad

Soon after he joined Digital Underground, Tupac started his own mentoring program, Underground Railroad. Once a week, Tupac spent time with a small group of young men. They read books, recorded raps, and went to movies together.

The original Underground Railroad was a secret network of people who helped slaves escape from the American South in the 1800s. The name of Tupac's program paid tribute to that memory. It also honored Shock G of Digital Underground. "He had faith in me when nobody cared," Tupac said in 1991. "That's the most beautiful thing you can do for a human being."

Song" was short. But the other Digital Underground members were impressed by how much meaning he could pack in. Still, *Vibe* magazine's Danyel Smith wrote, "Tupac felt he had more to say."

"Same Song" appeared on Digital Underground's 1991 record *This Is an EP Release*. An EP, short for "extended play," usually has five to eight songs. "Same Song" was also on the sound track for *Nothing but Trouble*, a film directed by Dan Aykroyd. *Nothing but Trouble* was Tupac's first movie. He and

First movie: Tupac and Digital Underground appeared in *Nothing but Trouble*, starring Chevy Chase, Dan Aykroyd, John Candy, and Demi Moore.

the rest of Digital Underground played themselves. In the film, the group is pulled over for speeding. They appear before a judge (played by Aykroyd). After they perform "Same Song"—with the judge joining in on keyboards—they are allowed to go.

Digital Underground's appearance was one of the highlights of *Nothing but Trouble*. But the film got bad reviews. "It's nothing but trouble and agony and pain and suffering and . . . bad taste," one reviewer wrote. Still, it was a start for Tupac.

Big Breaks

During this time, Tupac was writing and recording material for a solo album. He planned to release it under his stage name, 2Pac. Gregory tried to convince TNT/Tommy Boy, Digital Underground's record label, to sign Tupac. But the label chose not to do so. Finally, the label Interscope took a chance on him. Tupac's debut album was set for release in November 1991. Tupac was twenty years old.

Around the same time, Tupac broke into acting. In late 1991, he was in New York touring with Digital Underground. Money-B had an audition for the film *Juice*, directed by Ernest Dickerson. Tupac asked if he could come along and try out too. Money-B didn't get a part. But Tupac was cast as Roland Bishop. It was an important supporting role.

Tupac's rapid successes in both music and acting meant a lot to him. But one simple goal was even more important. By the end of 1991, Tupac had earned enough money to rent his first apartment.

Group effort: Tupac *(left)* and other members of Digital Underground give an interview in August 1991.

Vibe

Vibe magazine was founded by musician and composer Quincy Jones in 1993. It was one of the first magazines to focus on hip-hop music, much like *Rolling Stone* and others focused on rock. After Tupac's death, *Vibe*'s editors collected the stories about him into a book, *Tupac Shakur: 1971–1996*. It appeared on the *New York Times* newspaper's Best Seller List. *Vibe* ended publication in 2009 due to financial troubles, but a relaunch of the magazine is expected soon.

Until then, Tupac had usually slept on the floors in band members homes. He even spent nights on recording studio couches.

Tupac's apartment was a small one-bedroom place in Oakland, California. At the time, parts of "Coke-land" (nicknamed because so many people there used cocaine) weren't safe. But Tupac was deeply proud of his new home. "Tupac showed us all around," Danyel Smith wrote in *Vibe*. He pointed out his new dishes, new silverware, new sheets, and towels. "[He was] telling us without telling us of his profound relief at having a place of his own." Tupac had put up with years of being homeless. Having a home of his own meant more than he could say.

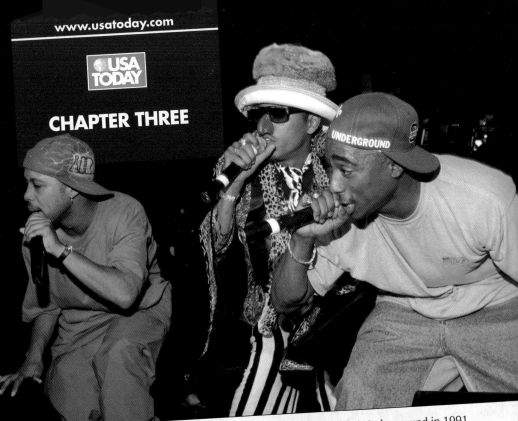

USA TODAY

CHAPTER THREE

Rebel of the Underground: Tupac (*right*) performs with Digital Underground in 1991. Members of Digital Underground helped Tupac make his first solo album.

A Thug's Life

Tupac's first solo album, *2Pacalypse Now*, hit record stores late in 1991. The album title was a cross between his stage name and the 1979 Vietnam War film *Apocalypse Now*. The word *apocalypse* refers to "the end of the world." *2Pacalypse Now* showed the influence of Digital Underground's members. They had helped Tupac make the record. One song was titled "Rebel of the Underground," his Digital Underground nickname. Another song, "Trapped," featured Shock G as a background rapper.

Apocalypse Now, directed by Francis Ford Coppola, was a 1979 film about the horrors of the Vietnam War (1957–1975). The movie appealed to Tupac, who wanted to show people the horrors of urban life.

But Tupac's solo material was different from Digital Underground's goofy party songs. *2Pacalypse Now* was clearly influenced by N.W.A.'s album, *Straight Outta Compton*. Like *Straight Outta Compton*, *2Pacalypse Now* was gangster rap. It was full of angry rhymes about urban life. It also took aim at the police. "Trapped," for example, accuses the

IN FOCUS

Straight Outta Compton

Straight Outta Compton, released in 1988 by N.W.A. (Niggaz with Attitude), is thought of as the first gangster rap album. The songs' lyrics were too violent to be played on the radio. The Federal Communications Commission (FCC) controls what kind of content can be broadcast on public airwaves. N.W.A.'s music was too harsh for FCC standards. But even though the music wasn't on the radio, the album still sold more than three million copies.

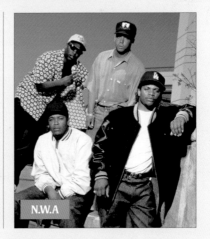

N.W.A

Gold record: Tupac's first album sold more than five hundred thousand copies. The most popular song on *2Pacalypse Now* was "Brenda's Got a Baby." He is shown here performing in 1991.

police of singling out black men. In the song, Tupac raps that black men can hardly walk around without the police going after them. In the song's chorus, Tupac repeats over and over again that "they" have him trapped.

Tupac's first single, "Brenda's Got a Baby," was even bleaker. It tells the story of a twelve-year-old girl who gets pregnant. After she gives birth, she throws the baby in the garbage. When the baby cries, Brenda comes back and brings the baby home. But her family soon kicks her out. Brenda tries to support her child by selling crack. Later, she sells herself for sex. In the end, she is murdered.

The song was very powerful. Many wondered if it was about someone Tupac knew. "No, she ain't somebody I know," he told *Vibe*. "She's one a them girls we all know." "Brenda's Got a Baby" made it to number three on the rap charts. The song helped *2Pacalypse Now* go gold (sell more than five hundred thousand copies).

The music industry gives honors to artists based on the number of albums sold. A gold album sells five hundred thousand copies or more. A platinum album sells one million or more. For two million copies sold, an album gets double platinum status. For three million, triple platinum.

Trapped

When Tupac wrote "Trapped," he had never been arrested or harassed by police. But that changed in the fall of 1991. On an October day, police stopped Tupac in downtown Oakland. They had seen him jay-walking (crossing the street against the light). At first, Tupac gave the police no problems. He showed the officers three forms of ID. But the two officers did not believe Tupac Shakur was his real name.

By the bay: Oakland is a city close to San Francisco. They are both on San Francisco Bay. Tupac lived in Oakland in the early 1990s.

Tupac began to lose patience. He asked why it took two officers to stop him for jaywalking. Oakland, after all, had a high rate of serious crime. Jaywalking didn't seem like that big of a deal. Finally, Tupac lost his temper and swore at the officers. They put him in a choke hold and knocked him to the sidewalk. "I woke up cuffed up, with my face in the gutter with a gang of people watching me like I was the criminal," he recalled.

Tupac spent seven hours in jail before the police released him. He missed the debut of his video on the popular hip-hop television show *Yo! MTV Raps*. In December of 1991, Tupac filed a ten-million-dollar lawsuit against the Oakland police. The case was settled for forty-two thousand dollars.

"No Place in Our Society"

Tupac was still just twenty years old when his first film, *Juice*, came out in January of 1992. His character, Bishop, was a troubled man with anger problems. In the film, Bishop gets a group of friends to rob the

Juice: Tupac's first major role in a movie was in *Juice*. Tupac *(center)* starred with Michael Badalucco *(left)* and Rony Clanton in the film.

corner store. Things go wrong when Bishop shoots and kills the store's owner. The film got mixed reviews. The *Washington Post* called it "passable but rather routine." But several critics noted Tupac's strong performance.

Tupac enjoyed the fame he got from *2Pacalypse Now* and *Juice.* "I loved the fact that I could go to any ghetto and be noticed and be known," he said. But his success in *Juice* had a bad side. He had played the part so well that many people began to think he wasn't acting. Tupac was not just a gangster rapper, they thought. He must be an actual gangster.

In April of 1992, Tupac's gangster image began to cause him problems. A young man in Texas, Ronald Ray Howard, shot and killed a state trooper. Afterward, officers found a copy of *2Pacalypse Now* in Howard's tape deck. Howard was facing the death penalty. To save Howard's life, his lawyer tried to blame Tupac. He claimed that Tupac's music had caused Howard to shoot the trooper. The lawyer singled out one lyric from "Soulja's Story." In the song, Tupac raps that he would rather shoot a cop than let one shoot him.

A few months later, Vice President Dan Quayle spoke out against Tupac's music. He said *2Pacalypse Now* was helping to destroy U.S. values. Quayle asked Interscope to pull Tupac's album from store shelves.

Not a fan: Vice President Dan Quayle, shown in 1991, thought Tupac's music was bad for society.

"This music has no place in our society," he said. Tupac was amazed that Quayle even knew who he was. In time, Tupac decided to embrace his new gangster image. Gangster rap was more popular than ever. Rap based on political issues was less popular. Twenty-one-year-old Tupac responded to this shift and helped make it happen.

In one interview, Tupac compared his lyrics to the television coverage of the Vietnam War. The Vietnam War was the first conflict to receive massive, in-depth coverage on television news in the United States. The U.S. public had never watched real war as it happened. Many scholars have claimed that the U.S. reaction to the TV coverage helped turn people against the war. Similarly, Tupac said, "I'm going to show the most graphic details [of ghetto life] and hopefully they'll stop it—quick."

Keeping It Real

Tupac had never been in a gang when he was growing up. He often said that before he made a record, he never had a record. By this, he meant he hadn't had a criminal record. But the line between his life and his art was blurring. In the hip-hop world, authenticity—keeping it real—was important. Many of Tupac's fans expected him to get into trouble.

When he moved to California, Tupac had dressed like the art student he'd recently been. But as he became more famous, he adopted a tougher look. His style included a head rag, sweatshirt, low-slung jeans, a nose stud, earrings, and a Rolex watch. In 1992 Tupac had *Thug Life* tattooed on his stomach. The *i* in *Life* was a rifle bullet. Tupac also collected guns. "You can't survive out here by yourself," he said. "The police ain't nothing but a gang. The National Guard is a gang. Somebody get a gun, the government get a bigger gun."

In August of 1992, things took a tragic turn. Tupac returned to Marin City for its fiftieth-anniversary festival. He got into a fight with some people in his old neighborhood. The conflict ended in gunfire. No one directly involved in the fight was hurt. But Qa'id Walker-Teal, a six-year-old boy playing in a nearby school yard, had been shot and killed by a stray bullet from the fight.

IN F⊙CUS

Cultural Graffiti

Tupac had many tattoos. Most famously, the words *Thug Life* were inked in large letters across his stomach. *Outlaw* and Christ with a crown of thorns were on his right arm. A snake was on his right shoulder. *Playaz* was on the back of his neck. A German cross with *Exodus 18:11,* "Now I know that the Lord is greater than all gods . . . ", was across his back. There were many more. One critic compared Tupac's back to how record samples sound. He pointed out that ideas, like the music, overlapped and bumped into one another.

Tattoo: Tupac shows off his Thug Life tattoo.

Tupac had not fired the gun. But the boy's family still filed a lawsuit against him and Interscope. The case was settled out of court for a reported three hundred thousand to five hundred thousand. Tupac later said the shooting haunted him. He deeply regretted being part of the accident.

"Tupac felt that he had to live the life that he sang about in his songs," Michael Eric Dyson, a professor who wrote a biography of Tupac, said in the film *Thug Angel.* "That's great when it's applied to gospel music, terrible when it's applied to gangster rap." "It's not that we have the answers because we don't," Tupac said about himself and other gangster rappers. "We're just being who we are, being as truthful to ourselves as we can. It's beyond good and evil. It's a thug life."

IN FOCUS

Thug Life

Tupac often called himself a thug and said he was living a thug life. He said this was due to Legs's influence. "That's where the thug in me came from," he said. In response to his critics, he claimed that he didn't invent thug life. With his stepfather Mutulu Shakur, Tupac wrote the "Code of Thug Life." The code included twenty-six rules for thugs. (In this context, *thug* seems to mean "gang member.") It banned selling drugs to children or pregnant women. It forbade harming civilians or the elderly. The code also stood against helping the police. Tupac's mentoring program, Underground Railroad, eventually turned into a musical side project called Thug Life. He worked with young rappers from all over. In the early days, these included many from the East Coast.

Driven to Succeed

Tupac started to feel guilty about having gotten out of the ghetto when other people couldn't. His guilt only made him work harder. He would write and record three or four songs a day, sometimes more. "If something happened to him, he wanted to write about it right on the spot," Money-B of Digital Underground said. The rapper Notorious B.I.G. (Christopher Wallace) said that Tupac once got up to go to the bathroom. When he came back, he had written two raps.

Writing lyrics "was his air. That was his oxygen," Shock G said. If Tupac was unhappy with what he had written, he would not change it. He'd throw it out and start a new song. "He just poured it out. . . . He came in there and said it how he felt it." But Tupac didn't have the best work habits. He needed to be drunk, high, or both to write songs. Tupac's drugs of choice were marijuana (weed) and alcohol. At the time, Tupac did not believe he was addicted. But his old friend Jada Pinkett was not fooled. "His mind was never clear," she said.

Tupac's drug use also changed his vocal style. He smoked so much in the studio that he often gasped for breath and skipped words. Tupac's solution was to triple his vocals. He would record the same song three times. Then he'd mix (overlap) the three recordings. That way, every word was clear.

A Second Album

Tupac's second album, *Strictly for My N.I.G.G.A.Z.*, came out in February 1993. Like other gangster rappers, Tupac used the "n-word" often. Unlike other rappers, Tupac changed the ugly word. He turned it into an acronym, "N.I.G.G.A." He said it stood for "never ignorant, getting goals accomplished." *Strictly for My N.I.G.G.A.Z.* went on to sell more than one million copies.

The songs on *Strictly for My N.I.G.G.A.Z.* were just as conflicted as the title. Its biggest hit, "Keep Ya Head Up," was a salute to black women, especially single mothers. In the song, Tupac gave a shout-out to women on welfare. He said he cared about them, even if no one else did. According to Danyel Smith of *Vibe*, "On each of Tupac's albums, he included at least one song that [showed] the side of himself that believed in good." Despite its grim viewpoint, "Brenda"

Fan love: Tupac takes time to sign an autograph at a charity event in the mid-1990s.

was the "good" song of *2Pacalypse Now*. "Keep Ya Head Up" was the "good" song of *Strictly for My N.I.G.G.A.Z.*

Other songs on the album undercut this good message. "I Get Around" was about irresponsible sex. The song featured Shock G and Money-B from Digital Underground. But the very next track, "Papa'z Song," shows a child's view of this behavior. In the song, Tupac rapped that his mother was the only one who stuck around. His father had left them with no money. Tupac's stepbrother, Mopreme (son of Mutulu Shakur), rapped with him on the song. Mutulu had left both of them during the years he hid from the FBI. "Everybody got a good side. Everybody got a bad side," Mopreme said. "Just Pac's was amped up a little bit more." Many of Tupac's friends and fans shared Mopreme's view. But Tupac did not. "People who think I'm like two different people—a wild gangsta and a caring, sensitive young black man—don't really know me," he said.

Meanwhile, Tupac's behavior continued to make headlines. In March of 1993, he was arrested for threatening a limousine driver in California. In April he was jailed for ten days in Michigan for attacking a local rapper with a baseball bat.

Poetic Justice

Tupac's second film was supposed to have been *Menace II Society*. The film was about a young man trying to survive the rough housing projects of Watts, a neighborhood in Los Angeles, California. The directors of *Menace II Society* were young twin brothers Allen and Albert Hughes. They had made some of Tupac's videos. But after Tupac

Menace II Society (1993) was the feature film debut of Tupac's old friend from BSA, Jada Pinkett. Pinkett later appeared in films such as *Ali* (2001) and *The Matrix Reloaded* (2003).

Directing brothers: Filmmakers Allen *(left)* and Albert Hughes directed the 1993 movie *Menace II Society.*

had several fights with them, they kicked him out of the cast. Tupac claimed they didn't even inform him personally. He first heard about his firing on MTV.

Tupac was angry. He stormed the set of a video that the Hughes brothers were filming. Armed once again with a baseball bat, he went after both twins. "That's a fair fight, am I right?" Tupac said. "Two [people] against me?" He was arrested for assault. Allen Hughes also filed a lawsuit against him. Once again, it was Tupac's behavior—not his talent—that was making headlines.

Instead of *Menace II Society*, Tupac's second film was *Poetic Justice*. It came out in July of 1993. Tupac had just turned twenty-two. Singer Janet Jackson played the lead character, named Justice. She's a hairstylist who dreams of becoming a poet. Tupac's character, Lucky, is a mail carrier and single father who wants to be a rapper.

Poetic Justice was director John Singleton's second film. Singleton was exactly the type of director Tupac wanted to work with. His first

Moviemaker: John Singleton directed Tupac in *Poetic Justice*. Singleton grew up in south central Los Angeles, and the themes of his movies are often drawn from his childhood.

film, *Boyz n the Hood* (1991), had been nominated for two Oscars. Like the Hughes brothers, Singleton was a young African American. He made movies about the inner city. On the set, Tupac's relationship with Singleton was similar to the one he had with Shock G. "We'd argue, then make up," Singleton said.

Tupac's character, Lucky, was the male lead. But Tupac thought the character was poorly written. In speaking his lines and giving his performance, he tried to give Lucky the depth that the script lacked.

 Poetic Justice (1993) featured an appearance by the well-known African American poet Maya Angelou. She is also the author of the poetry that Janet Jackson's character writes in the film.

July 23, 1993

The unbalanced scale of *Justice*

From the Pages of
USA TODAY

Poetic Justice casts Janet Jackson as a poetry-loving beautician named Justice (mom was in law school) who finds love in a mail truck with a postal homeboy named Lucky. *Justice* may be the loopiest high-profile entry in black cinema since Prince's own sophomore slump, *Under the Cherry Moon*. A disorienting opener hints at this: a movie-within-a-movie featuring Lori Petty (black-wigged) and Billy Zane (Yul Brynner pate [head]). We are, it turns out, at the drive-in from Hell, about to witness the gang-killing of Jackson's boyfriend.

From here on, Jackson is seeking love in an alien environment.

Poetic Justice: Tupac, shown with costar Janet Jackson, received good reviews for his acting in *Poetic Justice*.

Mom's dead, grandma is dead, and her mentor-boss (Tyra Ferrell in a great "fox" turn) prefers money to men. Meanwhile, a best pal already boozes, the latter's honey is a posturing lout, and police helicopters interrupt Jackson's home-alone solace.

Jackson, shorter and rounder than most female leads, is a refreshing presence, but it's tough to tell if she can act; if anything, *Justice* is stolen by *Juice*'s Tupac Shakur as Lucky, whose family woes contribute a few good scenes. Weird enough to attract vicious brickbats but also a tiny cult, *Justice* will likely find most viewers scratching their heads.

—Mike Clark

Costars: Stars Janet Jackson and Tupac experienced some personal tensions on the set of *Poetic Justice*.

Many critics noticed. "Shakur's Lucky is movingly complex," Robert Faires wrote in the *Austin Chronicle*. "In his shrugs and sighs are the hundred wrestling feelings of a man with dreams fighting to hang on."

Janet Jackson was well aware of Tupac's rough past. She had asked that he take an AIDS test before filming their on-screen kiss. Tupac was hurt that Jackson would be worried about catching AIDS from him. (AIDS cannot be spread by kissing.) Perhaps because of that demand, the costars had no spark. Still, the film got mostly good reviews. One *Washington Post* writer called it "often graceful, sometimes brilliant." For the positive role he played, Tupac was nominated for an Image Award by the National Association for the Advancement of Colored People (NAACP). It was a new experience for a self-proclaimed thug.

www.usatoday.com

USA TODAY

Life

SECTION D

January 2, 1991

'Gangsta' rap reflects an urban jungle

From the Pages of USA TODAY

Born in Los Angeles' gang-torn streets, gangsta rap portrays itself as the 6 o'clock news put to vinyl. The music crackles with gunfire. As gangsta pioneers N.W.A. say in "Gangsta, Gangsta": "I got a shotgun, and here's the plot/takin' (expletive) out with a flurry of buckshots." Are they street heroes or negative role models? For a frustrated generation of inner-city youth, they're both. "It's negative in a way, but it lets you know what's going on in reality," says Kevin Lee, 19, of Lake Arbor, Md. "In that sense, it's positive."

Jamie Brown publishes *Sister to Sister*, a Washington, D.C.-based magazine that covers rap and R&B. She became concerned when one of her two teen sons playfully pointed a finger at her head and recited lyrics from Kool G Rap and D.J. Polo's Streets of New York: "I also have a .38." "I don't even think it's music," Brown says. "It preaches disunity between black males and females, and harming one another physically. Brown has been printing gangsta rap lyrics in her magazine to show parents what their children are hearing. "What bothers me is that it's really their reality," Brown says. "When I saw N.W.A., I thought 'Our children are going through this?' It's good people are made aware of it, but not the kids." But that's what the kids want to hear, Ice T says. "My stuff is not for the squeamish or very prudish. It is for street people who hang out."

—James T. Jones IV

Troubling times: Tupac moved to Atlanta, Georgia, in 1993, but trouble followed him. He was accused of shooting two off-duty police officers not long after moving there.

From Prison to Death Row

■■■■■

By 1993 Tupac was one of rap's biggest stars. As his popularity grew, so did his police record. Still, he had never been accused of a serious crime. Ten days was the longest jail sentence he had ever served. But in the space of three weeks, that changed.

His manager had noticed that Tupac's life was getting out of control. He had talked Tupac into buying a home in Atlanta, Georgia. This southern city is a center for African American business, politics, and music. Tupac agreed that the slower, calmer pace of life in Atlanta would be a good change.

But the change didn't work out as planned. On October 31, 1993, just days after moving to Atlanta, Tupac was arrested again. This time, the charge was serious—aggravated assault. He was accused of shooting brothers Mark and Scott Whitwell. They were both off-duty police officers. The Whitwells claimed that after a traffic dispute, Tupac opened fire. Tupac argued he had stopped his car after he saw the Whitwells harassing an African American driver. When one of the officers drew a gun, Tupac fired in self-defense.

Soon the Whitwells' story began to fall apart. Several witnesses said Mark Whitwell had been the first to pull a gun. Worse still, the Whitwells' guns had been stolen from a police locker. Both officers

New hometown: Tupac moved to Atlanta, Georgia, on the advice of his manager. They thought life in the South would be a good change.

may have been drunk. And in their report on the incident, they had used a racial insult to describe Tupac and his friends. Seven months after the shooting, Mark Whitwell quit the force. The charges against Tupac were dropped.

After this incident, many of Tupac's fans thought of him as almost superhuman. Not only had he shot two white police officers, he had gotten away with it. He had not even gone to trial. That was hard to believe. "Shooting cops? And living to tell the story? And beating the rap? He was beyond real," Danyel Smith said in *The Vibe History of Hip Hop.*

More Trouble

A few weeks later, Tupac made the news again. He was in New York working on a basketball movie called *Above the Rim*. On November 14, 1993, Tupac met a nineteen-year-old woman at a dance club. Several days later, the woman came to visit Tupac at his hotel. What happened after that is unclear. The woman later told police that Tupac and three friends had raped her. Tupac did not deny that she had been raped. But he said that he had left the room before the rape occurred.

Scene of the alleged crime: A nineteen-year-old woman was sexually assaulted in Tupac's room at the Hotel Parker Meridien in New York.

Under arrest: Tupac is led from a Manhattan (New York) police precinct after being arrested in November 1993.

Tupac was arrested. He was charged with several crimes, including sexual assault and sexual abuse. On the night of his arrest, he was defiant. "I'm young, black. . . . I'm making money and they can't stop me," he said. "They can't find a way to make me dirty, and I'm clean." Once again, Tupac was front-page news. Many of the articles spoke out against Tupac and gangster rap. "For years, these rappers have been preaching drug culture and violence," a California politician said in a *New York Times* article. "But now they are openly living that life style. . . . That will have a [bad] effect on our young people who [imitate] the way these rappers dress, talk, and act." Similarly, the headline of a *Newsweek* article asked, "When Is Rap 2 Violent?"

Kevin Powell of *Vibe* saw things from Tupac's viewpoint. "I look at Tupac and I see myself, my homeboys, all the brothers I've ever [known], trying to prove ourselves to the world," he wrote. "But I wonder why Tupac's efforts . . . are so destructive. Over the past several months, as the media reported one violent incident after another, many people asked, 'Is Tupac on a self-destructive mission? Does he have a death wish? Is he crazy?'"

Tupac was released on bail. He was set to stand trial the next year. At the same time, John Singleton had planned to cast the twenty-two-year-old Tupac as the lead in his next film, *Higher Learning.* Singleton and Tupac had already worked together once, on *Poetic Justice.* After Tupac's arrests in Atlanta and New York, producers forced Singleton to drop him. Tupac's gangster image helped sell gangster rap records. But it did not work in Hollywood.

In March 1994, *Above the Rim* was released. Tupac's character, a drug dealer named Birdie, was "a standard cliché," reviewer Roger

Moviemaking: Tupac *(front, second from right)* played a drug dealer in the 1994 movie *Above the Rim.* It told the story of a high school basketball player struggling with life decisions.

Ebert wrote in the *Chicago Sun-Times*. However, Ebert wrote, "Shakur plays him well, and he makes a satisfactory bad guy."

Tupac Shot

Tupac was twenty-three when his sexual assault trial began in November of 1994. He faced up to twenty-five years in prison. Tupac said that he was innocent. He claimed that the police were out to get him because of his antipolice lyrics. During the trial, Tupac's lawyers blamed his accuser for what had happened.

Meanwhile, Tupac was running short of money. His records were still selling well. But he had lawyers to pay. And because of all that had happened, many of his concerts had been canceled. Tupac started hiring himself out to rap on other rappers' records to earn extra money.

On the night of November 29, Tupac and three friends stopped by Quad Recording Studios in New York City. He had agreed to record a verse for the young East Coast rapper Little Shawn. Little Shawn had released one album, *The Voice in the Mirror*, in 1992, and was working on new material. Tupac felt nervous about it because he didn't know the rapper well. But he needed the fee. In the lobby of the building, two men pulled out guns. They shouted at the group to lie on the floor and give up their jewelry. Tupac grabbed for one of the guns. The men shot him five times. He was hit twice in the head, once in the left arm, once in the thigh, and once in the groin. Then the attackers took his diamond ring and gold chains.

His friends dragged Tupac into the elevator and up to the studio. First, Tupac wanted some marijuana. He smoked it and called his mother as his friends tried to slow down the bleeding. Then he called 9-1-1. The police arrived quickly. Among them was Craig McKernan, who had arrested Tupac for the rape the year before. Tupac said hello and called the officer by name. "Hey, Tupac, you hang in there," McKernan said.

East Coast vs. West Coast

Hip-hop was born in the early 1970s in New York. But in the early 1990s, gangster rap, which came out of California, began to take over. Los Angeles began to rival New York as a hip-hop capital.

An East Coast-West Coast rivalry began to develop. It was worse between New York's Bad Boy Records (run by Sean Combs) and L.A.'s Death Row (run by Marion "Suge" Knight). At first, the rivalry was mainly about money. But after Tupac was shot and mugged in 1994, the rivalry turned personal. Tupac claimed Combs and the Notorious B.I.G., who was signed to Bad Boy, had set him up. Before the shooting, Tupac and Biggie had been friends. There was never any proof for Tupac's claim. But he believed it. The shooting and mugging was never solved.

The rivalry grew worse after Biggie released the single "Who Shot Ya?" Biggie said the song was not about Tupac. But Tupac thought Biggie was making fun of him. In response, Tupac released the single "Hit 'Em Up" with his new side project, the Outlawz.

By the mid-1990s, the rivalry was almost as bad as gang warfare. Producer and rapper Andre Young (Dr. Dre) saw that the bad feelings were getting worse. He said, "Pretty soon [people] from the East Coast ain't gonna be able to come out here and be safe. And vice versa."

Rivalry: Tupac claimed that the rapper Notorious B.I.G. *(left)* and Bad Boy Records owner Sean "Puff Daddy" Combs *(front, second from right)* were behind his 1994 shooting.

Overnight Recovery

When Tupac awoke in Bellevue Hospital Center, he had another shock. "After I got shot, I looked up and there was this [person] who looked just like me," Tupac said. Sitting by his bedside was Billy Garland. The men looked so much alike that Tupac was sure Garland must be his father.

Garland had seen Tupac's face on a movie poster for *Juice*. The face on the poster was a mirror image of his own. When he heard about Tupac's shooting on the news, he came to visit. It was the first time Tupac and Garland had met.

Tupac was afraid that the attackers would come back to the hospital to finish him off. He had bodyguards posted outside his door. All the next day, Tupac continued to bleed heavily. At 1:30 P.M., he had surgery on his right leg to stop the bleeding. The surgery was over at 4 P.M. At 6:45 P.M., he checked himself out of the hospital against the advice of his doctors.

The next morning, December 1, Tupac showed up at his trial. The jury had no contact with the outside world. So they didn't know that Tupac had been shot. He didn't want them to think he was skipping a court date. "I knew I had to show up no matter

Back to court: Tupac was shot five times at a New York City recording studio on November 29, 1994. He arrived at court two days later, on December 1, 1994, in a wheelchair.

what," he said. Tupac arrived in a wheelchair. His left wrist was bandaged. His bandaged head was hidden under a knitted hat. His bandaged leg was under sweatpants.

Later, Tupac left the courtroom because his leg went numb. He needed medical help. He secretly checked into a different hospital under the name Bob Day. Despite his efforts to hide, he continued to get death threats by phone.

Tupac was too sick to return to court that day. He wasn't there when the jury gave its verdict. They found Tupac guilty of sexual abuse. But he was cleared of the more serious sexual charges and of weapons charges. The judge sentenced him to one and a half to four and a half years in prison out of a maximum of seven. Tupac always claimed he had not raped the woman. However, he was sorry that he hadn't done something to stop the rape. He said he should have made sure any woman in his hotel room was safe.

Tupac's overnight recovery from five gunshot wounds became legendary. The fact that he had been shot during his trial confirmed the

USA TODAY Snapshots®

The time for crime

Average sentence length by top offenses:
(in months)

Murder **189.3**

Kidnapping/hostage taking **149.3**

Robbery **79.6**

Drug trafficking **76.4**

Sexual abuse **75.4**

Source: U.S. Sentencing Commission

By David Stuckey and Alejandro Gonzalez, USA TODAY, 2007

ideas of both critics and fans. "For those who want gangsta rap off the market, he was living proof of the genre's [hatred of women] and violence," Jon Pareles wrote in the *New York Times*. "But for fans, he became the [perfect example] of street-tough 'realness.'"

December 2, 1994

Jury finds Shakur guilty

From the Pages of
USA TODAY

The day after being shot five times, rapper/actor Tupac Shakur was found guilty Thursday of sexually abusing a 21-year-old female fan in a New York hotel suite last November. The jury of nine women and three men convicted Shakur, 23, on three counts, but cleared him of more serious . . . charges. "We're ecstatic," said Shakur's lawyer, Michael Warren. The jury deliberated over three days and also convicted Shakur's road manager Charles Fuller, 24, on the same charges. Both men face up to seven years in prison. The attorneys are expected to return to court Monday to arrange a sentencing date.

Found guilty: Tupac leaves court in a wheelchair on December 1, 1994.

Shakur, who was shot during a robbery outside a recording studio, was not present to hear the verdict. Bandaged and in a wheelchair, he'd arrived in court earlier Thursday after leaving Bellevue Hospital against doctors' wishes. "I was also anxious to return to court as soon as possible in order to end the stress of the recent trial I'm involved in," Shakur said. Bullets struck his hand, groin and thigh and grazed his head. Shakur underwent surgery and left the hospital 18 hours later. "The frenzy being caused by my stay made it impossible for me to get any rest," he said.

—James T. Jones IV

Thug Life: Volume 1

Thug Life, Tupac's side project with young rappers, released its first album in October 1994. The lyrics on *Thug Life: Volume 1* were even darker than Tupac's solo material. "*Volume I* shows only one side of the so-called gangsta [mind]: getting paid and avenging for dead homies [close friends]," Cheo Hodari Coker wrote in *Vibe*, "There's little that [shows] the futility of all that violence, or the daily stresses that lead countless kids down this path."

Thug Life: Volume 1 was planned to be the first of a series of Thug Life albums. Tupac's plan was for the members of the group to change. He wanted to give unknown rappers their first big break. But for many reasons, no more albums were made.

Others in the hip-hop scene were not so sure this "realness" was very real. "He has portrayed the role of thug," Jeremy Miller of *Source* magazine said. "There's a line where it's reality, and not reality. I think he's right on the line."

Prison

Tupac began serving his sentence at Clinton Correctional Facility in Dannemora, New York, on February 14, 1995. He had always believed that at some point he would serve time in prison. Afeni, Legs, Mutulu, and so many others he knew had served time. As a young man, he had even told Leila Steinberg that prison would give him good material for his raps.

But the reality of prison was nothing like his fantasy. He went through bad withdrawal symptoms when he stopped smoking marijuana. The other inmates harassed him. One rumor said that Tupac was sexually assaulted in prison. In an interview with *Vibe*, Tupac strongly denied it. Once he had been able to write four songs a day.

In prison, he couldn't write lyrics at all. But he did write a screenplay called *Live 2 Tell*. It was about a drug lord who struggles to change his life.

Before he went to prison, Tupac told Jada Pinkett that he was going to give up thugging. He planned to get rid of all his guns and get a new set of friends. He even thought he might give up rap and focus just on acting. In a famous prison interview with *Vibe*, he made similar promises. "Thug Life to me is dead," he said. "If it's real, then let somebody else represent it, because I'm tired of it.... This Thug Life stuff, it was just ignorance. My intentions was always in the right place." Tupac also talked about how his lyrics affected others. "If you see everybody dying because of what you saying, it don't matter that you didn't make them die," he said. "It just matters that you didn't save them."

Behind bars: A guard tower of the Clinton Correctional Facility in northern New York State, where Tupac served his time

On April 29, 1995, Tupac married girlfriend Keisha Morris at the prison where he was serving time. Tupac had met Morris, a prelaw student, at a New York club in 1994. The marriage was later legally dissolved as if it had never existed. "I moved too fast," Tupac told *Vibe* in February of 1996. "I can only be committed to my work or my wife. I didn't want to hurt her. She's a good person. So we just took it back to where we were before."

Me Against the World

While Tupac was in prison, his third album, *Me Against the World*, was released. The album had been recorded before Tupac went to prison. It debuted at number one on one of Billboard's music charts. Tupac became the first recording artist to have a number one album while serving time in prison. Despite his situation, Tupac thought of the success of *Me Against the World* as "one of my career highs." Many critics have pointed to the paranoia (fear not founded in reality) that runs through Tupac's work. *Me Against the World* was the best example yet. In "Death around the Corner," Tupac admits what the cause might be. Smoking weed, he rapped, was making him paranoid. (Paranoia is a well-known side effect of smoking weed, or marijuana.) Tupac did have real reasons to feel fear. But drugs clearly made his fears worse.

Like most of Tupac's work, the album was partly about him. The first sounds on the album are pretend news reports of his shooting. In another song, he raps that he is not a rapist. A *New York Times* reviewer wrote about how real Tupac's work was. "As other rappers strive to prove their 'realness,' 2Pac has become a [true] outlaw, with bullet wounds and . . . prison sentence to prove it." The most famous single from the album is another one of his "good" songs. "Dear Mama" is a thank-you to Afeni for her hard work as a single mother. One critic pointed out that Tupac speaks more clearly on "Dear Mama" than any other song. It is as if he doesn't want his listeners to miss a single word.

In 1990 Afeni realized that her crack use was out of control. She moved back to New York and managed to kick her habit. She was clean by the time she went to work for Tupac in 1994.

The track's most famous lyric is also its most honest. In it, Tupac calls his mother a crack fiend as well as a black queen. In those two lines, Tupac declares his love for Afeni as well as his disappointment in her. Like his mother had been, Tupac was brutally honest. "Dear Mama" was the main reason that *Me Against the World* sold two million copies. It also showed his fans—especially his female fans—that he was not the monster the media said he was. Tupac was serving time for sexual abuse. But "Dear Mama," like "Keep Ya Head Up," showed a softer side.

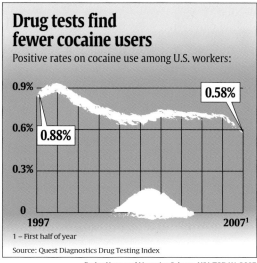

USA TODAY Snapshots®

Drug tests find fewer cocaine users

Positive rates on cocaine use among U.S. workers:

0.88%
0.58%

1997   2007[1]

1 – First half of year

Source: Quest Diagnostics Drug Testing Index

By Jae Yang and Veronica Salazar, USA TODAY, 2007

Death Row

Tupac's lawyers tried to get him released while they asked a judge for a new trial. But he could not raise the $1.4 million he needed for bail. That was when Marion "Suge" Knight, the head of Death Row Records, stepped in.

Knight visited Tupac in prison. He brought a contract to join Death Row Records. Knight offered to post the $1.4 million bail. The money was an advance on royalties (Tupac's share of the profits) on future albums. In exchange, Tupac would release three albums on the Death Row label. Tupac signed the deal. Tupac always said that he wanted to be on Death Row Records. But some people close to him felt that he had no choice in the deal.

On October 13, 1995, twenty-four-year-old Tupac walked out of prison. Knight sent a private jet to fly him back to California. That same night, Tupac was in the studio to record new music. By the next day, he had finished seven songs for his next album.

Tupac's work ethic hadn't changed. But something else had. Many of his old friends noticed the difference. "The light and the wit, the way that he would shine, it was completely changed, dimmed after that experience," Leila Steinberg said. Prison time had not given him endless material for raps, as he had hoped. Instead, Tupac told Steinberg, "Jail killed my spirit. It wore me out. I'm tired now. I don't know if I'm making any difference."

Death Row

Death Row Records was cofounded in 1992 by Suge Knight and Andre Young. Young was a member of the original gangster-rap group, N.W.A. Knight and Young had been childhood friends. Death Row's first release was Dr. Dre's *The Chronic* in 1992. By 1995 *The Chronic* had sold more than two million copies. In three short years, Death Row had become the biggest rap label in the country.

Knight was a smart, talented businessman. But he ran Death Row in a strange, sometimes violent way. In his office, he kept a fish tank with piranhas—aggressive meat-eating fish. He liked to feed them mice or rats. Knight had been convicted of various crimes, including assault with a deadly weapon. In 1995 he

Rapper Dr. Dre

was given five years' probation for beating two rappers with a gun as a punishment for using a studio phone. There were stories of many other violent incidents.

CHAPTER FIVE

Part of the gang: Tupac's first album for Suge Knight *(right)* at Death Row Records was *All Eyez on Me*, which celebrated the gangster lifestyle.

Tomorrow Is Not Promised

■ ■ ■ ■ ■

Tupac insisted he wasn't guilty of sexual abuse. And while in prison, he seemed to truly want to change his image. But after he signed with Death Row, all of his promises went away. Tupac's gangster image was worse than ever. Few of his fans or friends were surprised. Tupac's messages had always been in conflict. He had also always longed to fit in. His membership in Death Row was the closest Tupac had ever come to being in a gang. And if he wanted to be in the gang, he had to act like he was in the gang.

In an interview with a San Francisco radio station, Tupac said he had learned in prison that he couldn't change. "You know how they say, 'You've made your bed, now lay in it?' I tried to move. I can't move to no other bed. This is it." *All Eyez on Me*, Tupac's first album for Death Row, made his new commitment to the thug life clear. Prison hadn't made him a better person, Tupac rapped on "No More Pain." In fact, he had become even worse. The song ended with him shouting about thug life and the west side, meaning the West Coast.

All Eyez on Me was a double album. It included twenty-seven songs and was more than two hours long. The album featured more than a dozen guest rappers. Tupac said he named the album *All Eyez on Me*, "because they are. Everybody's watching for me to fall, die, get crippled, get AIDS, something."

 All Eyez on Me is often called the first rap double album. But this honor actually goes to DJ Jazzy Jeff and the Fresh Prince's *I'm the DJ, He's the Rapper*, released in 1988. The Fresh Prince is now better known as actor Will Smith. He is married to Jada Pinkett Smith.

Me Against the World had showed the gangster life as self-destructive. But *All Eyez on Me* celebrated it. Tupac raps about driving fancy cars, drinking, smoking, and chasing women. "2Pac glamorizes the gangster life for anyone who'll buy the fantasy," Jon Pareles wrote in the *New York Times*.

The album also renewed the East Coast-West Coast rivalry. On the cover, Tupac uses three fingers to make the *W* hand sign. He later said

February 12, 1996

2Pac keeps controversial 'Eyez' on ball

From the Pages of
USA TODAY

Expect all ears to be on *All Eyez on Me*, the snarling fourth solo album from Tupac Shakur, a.k.a. 2Pac. The double album is a thug-a-thon of hard beats, deep grooves, slick samples and tough raps about mean streets. Tuesday's release will be of keen interest to gangsta rap fans and detractors, plus nervous industry bean-counters and image-polishers.

2Pac began *Eyez* just after his October release from prison. After 11 months in jail, he posted $1.4 million bail and is free on appeal. Rife with profanity and gang imagery, *Eyez* arrives courtesy of controversial Death Row/Interscope, dumped by Time Warner last year and expected to ink a new distribution deal with MCA this week. While he was behind bars, 2Pac's *Me Against the World* sold 2 million copies after topping Billboard's pop chart for four weeks, the longest rap reign since SoundScan began tabulating in 1991.

Neither contrite nor converted, 2Pac pounds the gang tom-toms, celebrating misogyny and inner-city machismo. But the blaxploitation excesses are more cinematic and comical than threatening. Canny and versatile, 2Pac smoothly shifts from menacing to melancholy. He's sincere on "I Ain't Mad at Cha" and mischievous on "2 of Americaz Most Wanted," a duet with Snoop Doggy Dogg. In "California Love," a loping bragfest about rap's East/West coast rivalry, 2Pac scores one for his homey team.

— Edna Gundersen

that the *W* stood for "war." *All Eyez on Me* included the song "Wonder Why They Call U," with backup vocals by Faith Evans. Evans was Biggie's wife. To get at Biggie, Tupac said that he and Evans had had a sexual relationship. Evans strongly denied it.

The album went on to sell more than ten million copies. But not all critics liked it. One *Vibe* reviewer wrote that the album sounded "slapped together." He added, "*All Eyez on Me* is not the crime Pac has actually been convicted of, but it's pretty bad."

Frantic Pace

As ever, Tupac didn't just rhyme about the thug lifestyle. He also tried to live it. "Tupac . . . liked to stir up stuff and then watch it explode in others' faces," Dr. Dre said. "That's a hard way to live and a quicker way to die."

Tupac was living life on his own terms. But to his old friends, he didn't seem to be enjoying his

Working hard: In 1996 Tupac was busy with the release of his album *All Eyez on Me*, as well as acting in movies and shooting videos for songs released from the album. He is shown here at the Grammy Awards in February 1996.

success. "He wasn't so happy," Shock G recalled. "A lot of his laughter was forced. All those records, all he's talking about is the pain." According to Gobi, Tupac's friend and video director, Tupac surrounded himself with people. Yet, at times, he seemed to be very much alone. "Tupac seemed happiest when he was on a set or in the studio," Gobi wrote in his book, *Thru My Eyes: Thoughts on Tupac Amaru Shakur in Pictures and Words.*

Friend remembers: Tupac's friend and music video director Gobi poses with a photograph of the rap artist. Gobi released a book after Tupac's death about his personal and professional experiences with Tupac.

Tupac was working at a frantic pace. He would shoot a movie during the day. At night he'd work on a video. He and Gobi shot six big-budget music videos in a few months. Sometimes Tupac was so tired he would sleep in the limo between locations. If Tupac had any extra time, he would go to the studio. He recorded hundreds of tracks during this period. Tupac wanted to fulfill his contract with Death Row as soon as he could. He wanted to start his own projects. Gobi wasn't surprised. He said that people like Tupac are always in a hurry because they "know that tomorrow is not promised."

In public, Tupac expressed only deep loyalty to Death Row and Suge Knight. Tupac's relationship with Knight was almost like that of a father and son or of brothers. Knight often spoke of Death Row as being like a family.

Tupac finished three films after he got out of prison. All of them centered on the drug trade or drug use. In *Bullet* (1996), he played another bad-guy dealer. In *Gang Related* (1997), he and Jim Belushi played crooked cops who rob and murder drug dealers. In the black comedy *Gridlock'd* (1997), he and Tim Roth played drug addicts trying to quit.

Meanwhile, Tupac was setting up some projects of his own. He founded a film company, called 24/7, with Gobi and another partner. Tupac also set up his own production company, Euphanasia. The name combined the words *euphoria* (joy) and *euthanasia* (mercy killing). He even had plans to start his own record label, Makaveli Records.

Gang Related: Tupac starred in the movie *Gang Related*, which was released in 1997.

Fateful night: Knight *(left)* and Tupac attended a boxing match in Las Vegas on September 7, 1996. They are seen here attending a different boxing match in Las Vegas.

Trouble in Vegas

On September 7, 1996, Tupac was in Las Vegas for a boxing match between Mike Tyson and Bruce Seldon. The bout, held at the MGM Grand Hotel and Casino, lasted just two minutes. At 8:39 P.M., Tyson knocked Seldon out. At about 8:45, Tupac, Knight, and others from Death Row got into a fight of their own. Shortly after the match, they scuffled with Orlando Anderson. The reasons for the fight are unclear. Some people think Anderson was a member of a Los Angeles gang. He may have beaten up one of Tupac's bodyguards a few weeks before. Hotel security quickly broke up the fight. Tupac and his group left the building.

Later, Tupac met with Knight to go to his nightclub, Club 662. Tupac rode with Knight in Knight's 1996 black BMW. Ten other cars filled with Death Row employees and friends trailed behind them. At about 11:15 P.M., Knight's car stopped at a red light at East Flamingo Road and Koval Lane. A white Cadillac pulled up along the passenger side. Someone in the white Cadillac fired thirteen shots into Knight's car.

Tupac tried to climb to safety in the back seat. But he was hit four times. Two bullets hit him in the chest, one in the hand, and one in the leg. Knight made a U-turn and tried to flee. But he hit a road divider. Soon the police arrived. An ambulance took Tupac and Knight to the University Medical Center. Knight was treated for minor injuries to his head and was released.

 Tupac sometimes wore a bulletproof vest. But he left it off the night he was shot in Las Vegas.

Crime scene: The black vehicle in which Knight and Tupac were shot on September 7, 1996, in Las Vegas is seen behind crime scene tape.

September 10, 1996

Was Shakur victim in rap industry rivalry?

<u>From the Pages of</u>
<u>USA TODAY</u>

As Tupac Shakur had his right lung removed Monday in Las Vegas, speculation in the music world was whether his wounding was part of a competition between East Coast and West Coast music factions to sell records and dominate the rap world. Shakur remained in critical condition Monday at University Medical Center after being shot several times in the chest Saturday when he and Marion "Suge" Knight, head of Death Row Records, were driving to a nightclub.

L.A.-based Death Row, a label specializing in gangsta rap, boasts Shakur, Snoop Doggy Dogg, Hammer and others. They are rivals with Sean "Puffy" Combs, head of Manhattan's Bad Boy Entertainment, home of the Notorious B.I.G. Shakur has said that a 1994 incident in which he got shot five times was a set-up.

Police said Monday they had no suspects and were getting no cooperation from

At first, news reports about Tupac's condition differed. An Associated Press report said that his life wasn't in danger. Many of his fans thought Tupac would pull through. He had already survived the New York shooting, as well as a gun battle with Atlanta cops. Why should this time be any different?

Struggle for Life

Over the next two days, Tupac had two surgeries. The first was to remove his right lung. The second stopped internal bleeding. On the

Shakur's entourage. While the East-West rivalry is an initial theory for the shooting, *Vibe* magazine editor-in-chief Alan Light says he "wouldn't be surprised if it didn't have anything to do with Tupac, but is more related to Suge. There have been up to three contracts on his life at any given moment. He's very public . . . about his gang affiliation. There are a lot of people with a lot of issues with him."

Besides, Shakur was just in New York at the MTV video awards, and if this were a turf war, it's more likely something would have happened then, Light adds. In the September issue of *The Source*, Knight says, "Ain't no East coast/West coast thang. That ain't it."

West Coast: Snoop Doggy Dogg *(center)* and Tupac *(right)* were signed to Death Row Records. Knight *(left)* was the owner of the record label.

But Combs, in the September *Vibe*, says, "I'm ready for it to come to a head, however it gotta go down. . . . I just hope it can end quick and in a positive way, because it's gotten out of hand."

—Ann Oldenburg

third day, the doctors prescribed drugs to put him into a coma. They did so because he kept trying to get out of bed.

Gobi wrote emotionally about his visit to Tupac's hospital bed. "I saw his bandaged body covered by a thin white sheet, with tubes and machines . . . all over. Bandages covered his bullet wounds, and one of his fingers was missing. His head was swollen as a result of all the [drugs] they had pumped into him. I walked over and put my hand on his arm. It was cold. I said a prayer and walked silently out of the room."

Fight night: Tupac attended a boxing match in Las Vegas at the MGM Grand Hotel and Casino *(bottom right)* the night he was shot. One of the suspects in the shooting was a man Tupac and his friends fought with while at the boxing match.

For seven days, Tupac fought for his life. Outside the hospital, a crowd of well-wishers came and went. Rumors about the shooter ran wild. Some people thought the shooter may have been Anderson, the man Tupac and his friends had fought with at the MGM Grand. But hotel security staff had been talking to Anderson at the time of the shooting. Others thought Knight might have been the real target. But all the shots had been aimed at the passenger side. Another idea was that Tupac was killed as a warning to Knight or to get even with him. Yet another theory was that Tupac's shooting had come out of the East Coast-West Coast rivalry. The crime has never been solved.

November 7, 1996

Tales of a scary Knight

From the Pages of USA TODAY

Rapper Vanilla Ice is scared. Record promoter Doug Young has left the business. Music exec Jerry Heller carries a gun. The reason, according to Wednesday night's *PrimeTime Live*: Marion "Suge" Knight. Knight has been running his Death Row Records from an L.A. jail, where he is being held for violating probation.

PrimeTime's Brian Ross talked to Knight Tuesday about the night Tupac Shakur was shot. "What did you see?"

"Head shots."

"And then what?"

"Saw blood."

"If you knew who killed Tupac Shakur, would you tell police?"

"Absolutely not."

"Why not?"

"It's not my job. I don't get paid to tell on people."

Vanilla Ice (a.k.a Rob Van Winkle) told *PrimeTime* Knight took him to a balcony, made him look over as a threat and told him to sign over rights to his hit "Ice Ice Baby." Knight denies it. Says Ice, "I would never get on a witness stand and go against that guy 'cause you put a target on my forehead."

Scare tactics: Rapper Vanilla Ice (Rob Van Winkle) said that Suge Knight threatened him in 1990. Vanilla Ice is shown here in 2009.

Knight and other members of the Death Row group were of little help to the police. No one had seen the shooter. They'd only seen the white Cadillac. No one had seen its license plate number. And no other witnesses came forward with clues. "They were not quite [open]," Sergeant Kevin Manning of the Las Vegas Police Department said about Knight and his friends.

Rumors among the crowd gathered outside the hospital said that Tupac was getting better. For seven days, Tupac clung to life. But at 4:03 P.M. on Friday, September 13, he lost the fight. The official cause of death was a heart attack combined with breathing trouble.

Las Vegas hospital: Tupac died on September 13, 1996, at University Medical Center in Las Vegas *(shown above).*

Afeni Shakur chose to have her son's body cremated soon afterward. She didn't hold a funeral. Only a small private service held in Las Vegas took place. Tupac's family and friends later spread his ashes in the Pacific Ocean near Los Angeles.

Tupac's Books

Tupac read all the time. He left high school without a diploma. But he had read more books than many college graduates. Before his death, Tupac left his books with Leila Steinberg. Among his collection are:

The Art of War by Sun Tzu

The Catcher in the Rye by J. D. Salinger

Dictionary of Cultural Literacy: What Every American Needs to Know by E. D. Hirsch

I Know Why the Caged Bird Sings by Maya Angelou

In Search of Our Mothers' Gardens by Alice Walker

The Life and Words of Martin Luther King Jr. by Ira Peck

The Meaning of Masonry by W. L. Wilmshurst

Moby Dick by Herman Melville

Native Son by Richard Wright

The Odyssey by Homer

The Prince by Niccolo Machiavelli

Roots by Alex Haley

Sisterhood Is Powerful: An Anthology of Writings from the Women's Liberation Movement edited by Robin Morgan

The Souls of Black Folk by W. E. B. Du Bois

Tears and Laughter by Kahlil Gibran

Zen and the Art of Motorcycle Maintenance: An Inquiry into Values by Robert Pirsig

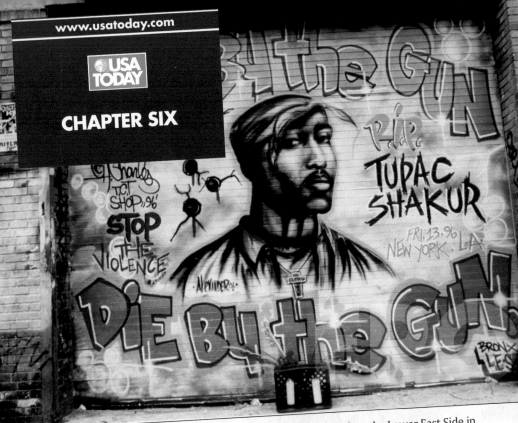

Tupac tribute: Tupac's death inspired a fan to paint this mural on the Lower East Side in New York City showing the rapper and the words "Live by the gun, die by the gun."

Resurrection

■■■■

Tupac's death hit his fans hard. For weeks, reporters were writing stories about it. The *New York Times*, for example, ran three major articles about Tupac on three separate days.

Tupac's death meant different things to different people. To fans who understood his pain, Tupac was a hero. To critics of gangster rap, his death proved that a link existed between music and violence. And to antiracism activists, Tupac's murder showed that the deck was stacked against African American men. No matter how rich or famous Tupac became, he was still just another young black man killed by gunfire.

"Tupac made people uncomfortable," Danyel Smith wrote in her obituary of Tupac in *Vibe*. "He was not trying to 'rise above' the way things are. He was not trying to 'be better.' No one ever said what would happen if folks got tired of aspiring to dignity. Tupac showed one way it already is."

Seven-Day Theory

Tupac's fifth solo album came out November 5, 1996, three weeks after his death. It was called *The Don Killuminati: The 7 Day Theory*. However, the album was not released under his usual stage name, 2Pac. This time, the artist was listed as Makaveli.

Posthumous album: The cover of Tupac's album *The Don Killuminati: The 7 Day Theory*, shows Tupac on a cross. The album was released under the name Makaveli.

Tupac's new name referred to Niccolo Machiavelli, an Italian writer of the 1500s. Machiavelli came up with the idea that the "ends justify the means." By this, he meant that a wrong action is sometimes necessary to achieve a greater good. "That's what got me here, my reading," Tupac told *Vibe* two weeks before his death. "It's not like I idolize this one guy Machiavelli. I idolize that type of thinking where you do whatever's gonna make you achieve your goal."

The album was dark from beginning to end. The cover showed Tupac on the cross. Behind him was a map of New York. "I'm on the cross bein' crucified for keepin' it real," Tupac said. On the album, Tupac's Makaveli character threatened to kill rivals like "the Notorious P.I.G."

IN FOCUS

Niccolo Machiavelli

Niccolo Machiavelli (1469–1527) was a political philosopher from Florence, Italy. His most famous book, *The Prince*, is a guide on how to become and remain a ruler. In the book, Machiavelli writes that lying, cruelty, and even murder are sometimes necessary to stay in power.

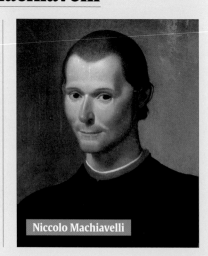
Niccolo Machiavelli

Six months after Tupac's death, the Notorious B.I.G. was shot and killed in Los Angeles. He was twenty-four years old. Biggie's murder has never been solved. His second album, *Life after Death*, came out two weeks after his death. Many people blamed the East Coast-West Coast rivalry for the losses of Biggie and Tupac.

Partly because of this album, some fans began to think that Tupac wasn't really dead. They thought the album gave clues that he was still alive. On November 25, rapper Chuck D of Public Enemy held a press conference in Atlanta. He gave a long list of facts about Tupac's death.

Niccolo Machiavelli had faked his own death to fool his enemies, Chuck D said. Maybe Tupac had done the same. Tupac had died on Friday the thirteenth. He was cremated quickly, without a public funeral. He almost always wore a bulletproof vest—except that night. The *Don Killuminati* cover art shows Tupac on the cross, as if he might come

Conspiracy theories: Rapper Chuck D *(above)* of Public Enemy believed Tupac could have faked his own death. Chuck D is shown here in 2007.

back from the dead. Finally, Chuck D said, "Suge Knight and Tupac are the only two people with the guts and a high enough profile to pull off a stunt like this."

The video for the song "I Ain't Mad at Cha" only fed the rumors. In the video, Tupac is shot five times. In heaven, he meets blues singer Billie Holliday, guitarist Jimi Hendrix, trumpet player Louis Armstrong, singer Marvin Gaye, and other African American legends. Tupac goes on to become a cigarette-smoking guardian angel. The video had been filmed a month before Tupac was killed.

In death, Tupac joined the small number of stars—such as James Dean, Marilyn Monroe, and Elvis Presley—who fans insisted were alive somewhere. Some writers pointed out that he was the first African American to inspire this belief. Rapper Big Syke once joked that Tupac had become the "ghetto Elvis."

"It's amazing to me that some kids think that he's still alive," Karen Lee, Tupac's publicist and friend, said in the film *Thug Angel*. "It's almost funny to me. Because he couldn't have been quiet this long. There's no way in the world he could have been quiet this long."

IN FOCUS

The Outlawz

One of Tupac's side projects was a group called the Outlawz. He gave all the members nicknames based on the names of famous dictators. Big Syke, for example, was named Mussolini after the Italian dictator Benito Mussolini (1883–1945). Other members took on the names of various other dictators, alive and dead. Tupac, as Makaveli, was the only one not named after a dictator. "I had to get a book on Mussolini," Big Syke said. "And then I got to [studying] Machiavelli. How am I going to find out about him if I don't read?"

www.usatoday.com

USA TODAY

Life

SECTION D

April 3, 1997

Dead or alive? Shakur survival rumors aren't laid to rest

<u>From the Pages of USA TODAY</u>

There are those who believe that Tupac Shakur did not die in Las Vegas last September after four bullets hit him in a drive-by shooting. There are those who believe that he's still alive and may come back. Rapper Chuck D's 18 reasons are listed under the heading "Tupac Shakur: Is he really dead???" on the Internet. In the February *Vibe* magazine, writer Dream Hampton opined [said], "There's no fooling my homies: Tupac is still alive."

"We hear that all the time," says Jammin' Dave Michaels, morning DJ on 106 JAM (WEJM), a Chicago hip-hop station. "It's a very bad rumor." Why do some believe Tupac lives? Numerology [the study of how numbers influence a person's life]. Tupac was gunned down seven months after his *All Eyez on Me* CD was released. He was shot on Sept 7. His age (25) added up to 7 (2+5). Even his time of death, 4:03, adds up to to 7. The name of one of his albums: *The 7 Day Theory*.

The rapper used the name Makaveli on his last album. Machiavelli, an Italian philosopher, suggested faking one's death to deter enemies. Tupac always wore a bulletproof vest but for some reason didn't wear one the night he was shot. No pictures of him in the hospital were ever released. And he died on Friday the 13th. He was cremated the day after he died, before an autopsy could be conducted.

But Keith Clinkscales, CEO of *Vibe*, says that while "Tupac had a huge presence in the community that loved and respected him," his death was a "human tragedy," and that should not be forgotten. Rumormongering is unkind to the family, he says. "These are not comic-book heroes," he says. "These are real people."

—Ann Oldenburg; Kevin V. Johnson

Final Films

The last three films Tupac worked on came out after his death. *Bullet* had a small release in theaters during October of 1996. In this film, Tupac played a drug dealer. Some fans claimed *Bullet* was an overlooked gem. Many others said it deserved to be overlooked. The film received no major reviews.

Gridlock'd, a comedy about two drug addicts, came out in January of 1997. Film critic Roger Ebert called it Tupac's best performance. In the film, Spoon (Tupac) and Stretch (Tim Roth) try to find a rehab program before they lose the urge to quit. But again and again, they are blocked by paperwork and waiting lists. In one darkly funny scene, Spoon figures the only solution is to go to the emergency room. So he tries to persuade Stretch to stab him.

Gridlock'd: Tupac starred with actor Tim Roth *(right)* in one of his final films, *Gridlock'd*. The movie was released in 1997, after Tupac's death.

According to Janet Maslin of the *New York Times*, Tupac "could have looked forward to a big future on the screen." One line from the film jumped out at audiences. "Ever feel like your luck's running out, man?" Tupac says in an early scene. "Lately I feel like my luck's running out."

His final film, *Gang Related*, came out in August 1997. The *New York Times* critic faulted its complex plot. But others liked it. As usual, Tupac's acting was praised. "It [shows] again the tragic futility of the death of Tupac Shakur," Stephen Hunter wrote in the *Washington Post*.

Amaru Entertainment

When Tupac died, Afeni Shakur learned that his finances were a mess. During his short career, he had sold millions of albums. But somehow, he had ended up owing Death Row millions of dollars.

After a long legal battle, Afeni won the rights to Tupac's unreleased music. She formed the company Amaru Entertainment to release these songs and his other creative work. The first release was *R U Still Down? (Remember Me)*, a double CD of outtakes released in late 1997. This was followed by *2Pac's Greatest Hits* in 1998.

Like *All Eyez on Me*, *2Pac's Greatest Hits* sold more than nine million

Amaru Entertainment: Tupac's mother, Afeni *(above)*, won the rights to his unreleased music after his death. She formed the company Amaru Entertainment.

Overall, Amaru Entertainment has released twelve albums. This total is more than double the number Tupac put out when he was alive.

copies. Both are listed among the top one hundred best-selling albums of all time, according to the Recording Industry Association of America (RIAA). Tupac is also listed among the RIAA's top-selling artists.

Amaru has also released several albums of Tupac's live performances. Most of them sold well. But some critics weren't impressed. They wondered if Tupac would have thought that all the songs were good enough to release.

Tupac: Resurrection, the sound track to the film of the same name, came out in 2003. The film, also released in 2003, took a unique approach. The narration was done by Tupac. He had left behind many hours of taped interviews. Director Lauren Lazin was able to combine them so that Tupac told his own story from before his birth to beyond the grave. The film was nominated for an Oscar for best documentary.

Tupac: Resurrection: Director Lauren Lazin *(left)* and producer Afeni Shakur celebrate after the 2003 opening of the movie *Tupac: Resurrection*.

November 11, 2003

Resurrection book, film bring Tupac back

From the Pages of
USA TODAY

Seven years after his murder, hip-hop megastar Tupac Shakur is speaking for himself in a documentary movie and best-selling book. Shakur, who was shot and killed in Las Vegas at age 25, recently was listed by *Forbes* magazine as No. 8 on its list of money-earning dead entertainers.

His mother, former Black Panther activist Afeni Shakur, the keeper of her son's legacy, says the past seven years "have been extremely painful, watching and listening while others incorrectly attempted to define who my son really

In his own words: The film *Tupac: Resurrection* is narrated by Tupac, using interviews and other recordings made before his death.

was." She says she's not trying to change her son's image, "but I have an obligation to let him tell his story even if he is not here physically. The end result is in God's hands."

Tupac: Resurrection is designed as a "self-portrait of a cultural icon." Directed by Lauren Lazin, it's narrated by Shakur himself, using interviews, poetry performances, private home movies and never-before-seen concert footage. The soundtrack, with Eminem's single "Running (Dying to Live)," is out today. The companion book, *Tupac: Resurrection*, touted by its publisher as "the autobiography he never got to write," was published last month.

—Bob Minzensheimer

In memory: The Tupac Amaru Shakur Foundation in Georgia held a ceremony in honor of the slain rapper on the tenth anniversary of his death in 2006. The event included a planting ceremony in the peace garden, a drum ceremony, and a speech by Afeni Shakur.

In June of 2005, Afeni opened the Tupac Amaru Shakur Center for the Arts in Stone Mountain, Georgia. The center is based on the Baltimore School for the Arts. Teenagers can take classes in

Actor Anthony Mackie played Tupac in the 2009 film *Notorious*, a "biopic" about the life of the Notorious B.I.G.

Playing Tupac: Actor Anthony Mackie had a supporting role as Tupac in a 2009 movie about the rapper Notorious B.I.G., called *Notorious*.

writing, singing, acting, dance, and other creative fields. Profits from Tupac's recordings pay for the center. In some ways, the center is a strange memorial to a gangster rapper. It includes a six-acre (2.4 hectare) peace garden with a peace trail.

So far, legal battles have prevented a film biography of Tupac from moving forward. In 2009 Morgan Creek Entertainment filed a lawsuit against Amaru Entertainment. Morgan Creek claimed that Amaru backed out of a deal for the rights to a film about Tupac. Amaru sued back. Despite the conflict, Afeni hopes that someday a Tupac movie will be made. Meanwhile, a movie about Notorious B.I.G. did come out in 2009, in which Tupac was featured.

Tupac's Legacy

Tupac's career lasted just six years. Eleven months of that were spent in prison. During that small window of time, Tupac was highly productive. He released five solo albums and acted in six films.

Tupac's brief career has had a big impact on hip-hop and other forms of music. He has sold more than 75 million albums worldwide. Along with Eminem, he is one of the top two best-selling rap artists ever. Since his death, Tupac has had three number one songs. Fans and critics rank him as one of the greatest rappers of all time. So do fellow artists.

IN FOCUS

Tupac and Religion

Religion and God were frequent themes in Tupac's work, music professor Teresa Reed pointed out. An entire chapter of her book, *The Holy Profane: Religion in Black Popular Music*, is about Tupac. "Black slaves always likened their suffering to that of biblical figures," she wrote. Jesus on the cross, Daniel in the lion's den, and Jonah in the whale were common themes in African American slave songs. Similarly, Tupac "connects Christ's [pain] to his own" on songs such as "Hail Mary." Tupac believed in some higher power. "I try to pray to God every night," he once said. "Unless I pass out."

Hip-hop influence: Rap artists such as 50 Cent *(above)* are influenced by Tupac's music and attitude.

His work has been a major influence on countless hip-hop artists. Among them are Lil Wayne (Dwayne Carter, Jr.) and 50 Cent (Curtis Jackson). "Every rapper who grew up in the nineties owes something to Tupac," 50 Cent wrote in an essay for *Rolling Stone*. "People either try to [be like] him in some way, or they go in a different direction because they didn't like what he did. But whatever you think of him, he definitely developed his own style. He didn't sound like anyone who came before him."

After Tupac's death, many people wondered what he might have been able to do if he had not died so young. We can only guess what he might have achieved in music or acting if his life hadn't ended so young. "If Malcolm X died at 25, he would have been a street hustler named Detroit Red," Quincy Jones said. "If Martin Luther King died at 25, he would have been a local Baptist minister who had not arrived on the national scene. If I would have died at 25, I would have been known as a trumpet player

IN FOCUS

Tupac Goes to College

Since his death, Tupac's poetry and lyrics have been taught at several colleges. The University of California at Berkeley offered a class on Tupac. Student Arvand Elihu and professor Robert Brentano set up History 98: The Poetry and History of Tupac Shakur. Elihu led the class in discussions on Tupac's lyrics. "View him in [Middle Ages] terms," Elihu told the class. "Substitute the word 'sword' for 'gun' and see how his poetry takes on a whole new meaning." Afeni Shakur visited the class.

Harvard University held a one-day conference on Tupac and his work. It was called "All Eyez on Me: Tupac Shakur and the Search for a Modern Folk Hero." The University of Washington offered Comparative History of Ideas 270: 2Pac. In this class, students wrote their own rhymes and read Machiavelli and Shakespeare's *Hamlet* along with Tupac's poems.

and struggling composer—just a sliver of my life potential. "Tupac had often said he never expected to live to be thirty. "From the moment he was born, I measured his life in five-year periods," Afeni recalled. "When he was five, I was so grateful. When he was ten, I thanked God he was ten. Fifteen, twenty, twenty-five. I was always amazed he'd survived. He was a gift."

TIMELINE

1969 Afeni Shakur and twenty other Black Panthers are arrested and charged with planning to blow up buildings in New York City.

1971 Afeni and thirteen others are cleared of all charges. Tupac Amaru Shakur is born in New York.

1972 Tupac's godfather Geronimo Pratt is sent to prison for murder and kidnapping.

1983 Tupac appears in *A Raisin in the Sun* at Harlem's Apollo Theater.

1985 Tupac moves with his family to Baltimore, Maryland. He attends the Baltimore School for the Arts.

1988 Tupac is sent to live in Marin City, California, and begins attending Mount Tamalpais High School. Mutulu Shakur is sentenced to sixty years in prison for murder and armed robbery.

1989 Tupac meets Leila Steinberg, who becomes his first manager.

Tupac and his mother, Afeni

Tupac in 1993

1990 Tupac joins Digital Undergroud on tour as a roadie and dancer.

1991 Tupac raps on Digital Underground's "Same Song" and appears in *Nothing but Trouble*. Later, *2Pacalypse Now* is released and Tupac files a lawsuit against the Oakland police.

1992 Tupac appears in *Juice*. Dan Quayle criticizes Tupac's music. Tupac is involved in a Marin City gunfight where a stray bullet kills a young boy.

1993 *Strictly for My N.I.G.G.A.Z.* is released. Tupac is arrested multiple times for assault and charged with sexual assault and sexual abuse. Tupac stars in *Poetic Justice* with Janet Jackson.

1994 Tupac appears in *Above the Rim* and releases an album with Thug Life. He is shot five times in New York City but survives. Billy Garland visits Tupac in the hospital. Tupac is found guilty of sexual abuse.

1995 Tupac begins serving his prison sentence at Clinton Correctional Facility. He marries Keisha Morris while in prison, but the marriage ends shortly after. *Me Against the World* is released. Tupac leaves prison on bail and signs to Death Row Records.

1996 *All Eyez on Me* is released, and Tupac appears in *Bullet*. Tupac is shot four times in Las Vegas while with Suge Knight. He dies of related injuries one week later. *The Don Killuminati: The 7 Day Theory* is released in the month following Tupac's death.

1997 Afeni Shakur founds Amaru Entertainment. *R U Still Down?* (the first posthumous Tupac collection) is released. Tupac stars in *Gang Related* and *Gridlock'd*, his final films. Geronimo Pratt is released from prison after his trial is ruled to be unfair.

1998 *2Pac's Greatest Hits* is released.

2000 *The Rose That Grew from Concrete*, a spoken word collection of Tupac's poetry, is released.

Tupac recording

2002 Tupac makes *Forbes* magazine's list of top-earning dead celebrities.

2003 The *Tupac: Resurrection* documentary and album are released.

A statue of Tupac at the Tupac Amaru Shakur Center for the Arts

2005 The Tupac Amaru Shakur Center for the Arts in Stone Mountain, Georgia, opens.

2006 *The Guinness Book of World Records* lists Tupac as the best-selling rap artist ever.

2009 Actor Anthony Mackie plays Tupac in the film *Notorious*.

GLOSSARY

activist: a person who tries to bring about social or political change

apartheid: the legal policy of racial separation in South Africa from 1948 to 1994

authenticity: being "real" or genuine. Authenticity is an important value in the hip-hop world.

Broadway: a street in New York City that is famous for its theaters

conspiracy: a secret agreement to do something illegal

crack: a powerful form of the drug cocaine that is smoked rather than snorted

defendant: a person charged with committing a crime

gangster rap: a form of rap that focuses on the urban lifestyle, especially gang life

harassment: behavior that threatens or disturbs someone else

hip-hop: a type of popular music that often features rapping along with background music created by a DJ

homie: a close friend

hood: neighborhood

public aid: money the government gives to individuals or families who don't have enough money to pay for rent, food, and other needs

revolutionary: a person who fights for some kind of extreme social change

rivalry: an intense competition between two individuals or groups

roadie: a person who travels with a band and helps them carry and set up their equipment

FILMOGRAPHY

Nothing but Trouble
Released: 1991
Director: Dan Aykroyd

Juice
Released: 1992
Director: Ernest R. Dickerson

Poetic Justice
Released: 1993
Director: John Singleton

Above the Rim
Released: 1994
Director: Jeff Pollack

Bullet
Released: 1996
Director: Julien Temple

Gridlock'd
Released: 1997
Director: Vondie Curtis-Hall

Gang Related
Released: 1997
Director: Jim Kouf

DISCOGRAPHY

2Pacalypse Now
Label: Interscope
Released: 1991

Strictly 4 My N.I.G.G.A.Z.
Label: Interscope
Released: 1993

Thug Life: Volume 1 [with Thug Life]
Label: Interscope
Released: 1994

Me Against the World
Label: Interscope
Released: 1995

All Eyez on Me
Label: Death Row
Released: 1996

The Don Killuminati: The 7 Day Theory [as Makaveli]
Label: Death Row
Released: 1996

R U Still Down? (Remember Me)
Label: Amaru/Jive
Released: 1997

Still I Rise [with Outlawz]
Label: Amaru/Interscope
Released: 1999

Until the End of Time
Label: Amaru/Interscope
Released: 2001

Better Dayz
Label: Amaru/Interscope
Released: 2002

Loyal to the Game
Label: Amaru/Interscope
Released: 2004

Pac's Life
Label: Amaru/Interscope
Released: 2006

SOURCE NOTES

5 Cory Johnson, "Sweatin' Bullets," in *Tupac Amaru Shakur 1971–1996*, ed. *Vibe* (New York: Three Rivers Press, 1997), 41.

7 Kevin Powell, "Tupac Shakur 1971–1996," *Rolling Stone*, October 31, 1996, http://www.rollingstone.com/artists/215/articles/story/5938593 (January 21, 2010).

10 Michael Eric Dyson, *Holler If You Hear Me: Searching for Tupac Shakur* (New York: Basic Civitas Books, 2001), 30.

11 Ibid., 31.

12 Kevin Powell, "This Thug's Life," in *Tupac Amaru Shakur 1971–1996*, ed. *Vibe* (New York: Three Rivers Press, 1997), 22.

13 Ibid.

14 Ibid., 25.

14 Armond White, *Rebel for the Hell of It: The Life of Tupac Shakur* (New York: Thunder's Mouth Press, 1997), 1.

16 Powell, "This Thug's Life," 25.

16 Ibid.

17 White, 6.

18 Powell, "This Thug's Life," 25.

18–19 Ibid.

19 Ibid.

19 Ibid.

20 White, 13.

21 Powell, "This Thug's Life," 27.

22 Ibid.

23 Ibid.

25 Michael Small, *Break It Down: The Inside Story from the New Leaders of Rap* (New York: Citadel Press, 1992), 202.

26 Leila Steinberg, introduction to *The Rose That Grew from Concrete*, by Tupac Shakur (New York: Pocket Books, 1999), xx.

26–27 *Thug Angel*, DVD, directed by Peter Spirer (QD3 Entertainment, 2002).

27 Ibid.

27 Ibid.

28 Ibid.

30 Ibid.

30 Small, 202.

31 Danyel Smith, "Tupac Shakur," in *The Vibe History of Hip-Hop*, ed. Alan Light (New York: Three Rivers Press, 1999), 299.

31 Hal Hinson, "Nothing but Trouble," *Washington Post*, February 16, 1991, http://www.washingtonpost.com/wp-srv/style/longterm/movies/videos/nothingbuttroublepg13hinson_a0a9d6.htm (January 21, 2010).

33 Danyel Smith, "Home at Last," in *Tupac Amaru Shakur 1971–1996*, ed. *Vibe* (New York: Three Rivers Press, 1997), 129.

36 Smith, "Tupac Shakur," 298.

38 Small, 201.

39 Hal Hinson, "Juice," *Washington Post*, January 17, 1992, http://www.washingtonpost.com/wp-srv/style/longterm/movies/videos/juicerhinson_a0a733.htm (January 21, 2010).

39 Powell, "This Thug's Life," 29.

40 White, 78.

40 *Tupac: Resurrection*, DVD, directed by Lauren Lazin (MTV Networks and Amaru Entertainment, 2003).

40 *Thug Angel.*

41 Ibid.

41 White, 57.

42 Charisse Jones, "For a Rapper, Life and Art Converge in Violence," *New York Times,* December 1, 1994, A1.

42 Ibid.

42 Ibid.

42 Dyson, 240.

43 Danyel Smith, "Introduction," in *Tupac Amaru Shakur 1971–1996*, ed. *Vibe* (New York: Three Rivers Press, 1997), 17.

44 *Thug Angel.*

44 White, 169.

45 Powell, "This Thug's Life," 29.

46 *Vibe, Tupac Amaru Shakur 1971–1996* (New York: Three Rivers Press, 1997), 152.

48 Robert Faires, "Poetic Justice," *Austin Chronicle*, July 23, 1993, http://www.austinchronicle.com/gbase/Calendar/Film?Film=oid%3a139124 (January 21, 2010).

48 Desson Howe, "Poetic Justice," *Washington Post*, July 23, 1993, http://www.washingtonpost.com/wp-srv/style/longterm/movies/videos/poeticjusticerhowe_a0afdf.htm (January 21, 2010).

52   Smith, "Tupac Shakur," 301.

53   Powell, "This Thug's Life," 22.

53   Calvin Sims, "Gangster Rappers: The Lives, the Lyrics," *New York Times*, November 28, 1993, sec. 4, 3.

54   Alan Light, "Who's Gonna Take the Weight?" in *Tupac Amaru Shakur 1971–1996*, ed. *Vibe* (New York: Three Rivers Press, 1997), 33.

54   Powell, "This Thug's Life," 31.

55   Roger Ebert, "Above the Rim," *Chicago Sun-Times*, March 23, 1994, http://rogerebert.suntimes.com/apps/pbcs.dll/ article?AID=/19940323/REVIEWS/403230301/1023 (January 21, 2010).

56   Kevin Powell, "Live from Death Row," in *Tupac Amaru Shakur 1971–1996*, ed. *Vibe* (New York: Three Rivers Press, 1997), 77.

55   Cory Johnson, "Sweatin' Bullets," 41.

57   *Vibe*, 97.

57–58 Kevin Powell, "Ready to Live," in *Tupac Amaru Shakur 1971–1996*, ed. *Vibe* (New York: Three Rivers Press, 1997), 48.

58   Jon Pareles, "Prison Makes Rap Tougher," *New York Times*, February 13, 1996, C13.

60   Cheo Hodari Coker, "Thug Life, Volume 1," in *Tupac Amaru Shakur 1971–1996*, ed. *Vibe* (New York: Three Rivers Press, 1997), 37.

60   Jones, "For a Rapper, Life and Art Converge in Violence," A1.

61   Powell, "Ready to Live," 51.

61   Ibid.

62   Powell, "Live from Death Row," 79.

62   *Tupac: Resurrection.*

62   Jon Pareles, "Confessions of a Rapper Who Done Wrong," *New York Times*, April 9, 1995, http://query.nytimes.com/gst/fullpage.html? res=990CE7DC1E3EF93AA35757C0A963958260 (January 21, 2010).

65   Dyson, 215.

65   Ibid.

67   Michel Marriott, "Shots Silence Angry Voice Sharpened by the Streets," *New York Times*, September 16, 1996, A1.

67   Eithne Quinn, "'All Eyez on Me': The Paranoid Style of Tupac Shakur," in *Conspiracy Nation: The Politics of Paranoia in Postwar America*, ed. Peter Knight (New York: New York University Press, 2002), 189.

67   Pareles, "Prison Makes Rap Tougher," C13.

69   *Vibe*, 80.

69   Dyson, 169.

69   *Thug Angel.*

69   Gobi, *Thru My Eyes: Thoughts on Tupac Amaru Shakur in Pictures and Words* (New York: Atria Books, 2005), 98.

70   Ibid., 86.

75   Ibid., 150.

78   Rob Marriott, "All That Glitters," in *Tupac Amaru Shakur 1971–1996*, ed. *Vibe* (New York: Three Rivers Press, 1997), 121.

81   Smith, "Tupac Shakur," 305.

82   Marriott, 125.

82   Ibid.

84   *Vibe*, 152.

84   Ibid., 257.

84   *Thug Angel.*

84   Dyson, 100.

87   Janet Maslin, *New York Times*, January 29, 1997, http://movies2 .nytimes.com/mem/movies/review.html?_r=1&res=9E02E3D91E3A F93AA15752C0A961958260&oref=slogin (January 21, 2010).

87   Ibid.

87   Stephen Hunter, "Gang Related: Tupac's Triumph," *Washington Post*, October 8, 1997, http://www.washingtonpost.com/wp-srv/style/ longterm/movies/review97/gangrelatedhunt.htm (January 21, 2010).

92   Teresa L. Reed, *The Holy Profane: Religion in Black Popular Music* (Lexington: University Press of Kentucky, 2003), 155.

92   *Vibe*, 98.

93   50 Cent, "Tupac Shakur," *Rolling Stone*, April 21, 2005, http://www .rollingstone.com/artists/215/articles/story/7249932 (January 21, 2010).

93–94   *Thug Angel.*

94   Billy Jam, "Strictly for My Classmatez," in *Tupac Amaru Shakur 1971–1996*, ed. *Vibe* (New York: Three Rivers Press, 1997), 147.

94   Cathy Scott, *The Killing of Tupac Shakur* (Las Vegas, NV: Huntington Press, 1997), 182.

SELECTED BIBLIOGRAPHY

Dyson, Michael Eric. *Holler If You Hear Me: Searching for Tupac Shakur*. New York: Basic Civitas Books, 2001.

Gobi. *Thru My Eyes: Thoughts on Tupac Amaru Shakur in Pictures and Words*. New York: Atria Books, 2005.

Guy, Jasmine. *Afeni Shakur: Evolution of a Revolutionary*. New York: Atria Books, 2004.

Quinn, Eithne. "'All Eyez on Me': The Paranoid Style of Tupac Shakur." In *Conspiracy Nation: The Politics of Paranoia in Postwar America*. New York: New York University Press, 2002.

Reed, Teresa L. *The Holy Profane: Religion in Black Popular Music*. Lexington: University Press of Kentucky, 2003.

Shakur, Tupac Amaru. *The Rose That Grew from Concrete*. New York: Pocket Books, 1999.

Small, Michael. *Break It Down: The Inside Story from the New Leaders of Rap*. New York: Citadel Press, 1992.

Smith, Danyel. "Tupac Shakur." In *The Vibe History of Hip Hop*. Edited by Adam Light. New York: Three Rivers Press, 1999.

Thug Angel. DVD. Directed by Peter Spirer. QD3 Entertainment, 2002.

Tupac: Resurrection. DVD. Directed by Lauren Lazin. MTV Networks and Amaru Entertainment, 2003.

Vibe. Tupac Amaru Shakur 1971–1996. New York: Three Rivers Press, 1997.

White, Armond. *Rebel for the Hell of It: The Life of Tupac Shakur*. New York: Thunder's Mouth Press, 1997.

FURTHER READING AND WEBSITES

Books

Alexander, Frank. *Got Your Back: Protecting Tupac in the World of Gangsta Rap.* New York: St. Martin's Press, 2000.

Ardis, Angela. *Inside a Thug's Heart.* New York: Dafina Books, 2009.

Bastfield, Darrin Keith. *Back in the Day: My Life and Times with Tupac Shakur.* Cambridge, MA: Da Capo Press, 2003.

Brill, Marlene Targ. *America in the 1990s.* Minneapolis: Twenty-First Century Books, 2009.

Brown, Sam. *Tupac: A Thug Life.* Medford, NJ: Plexus Publishing, 2005.

Bynoe, Yvonne. *Encyclopedia of Rap and Hip-Hop Culture.* Westport, CT: Greenwood Press, 2006.

Chang, Jeff. *Can't Stop, Won't Stop: A History of the Hip-Hop Generation.* New York: St. Martin's Press, 2005.

Doeden, Matt. *Will Smith: Box Office Superstar.* Minneapolis: Twenty-First Century Books, 2010.

Donovan, Sandy. *The African American Experience.* Minneapolis: Twenty-First Century Books, 2011.

Finlayson, Reggie. *Nelson Mandela.* Minneapolis: Twenty-First Century Books, 1999.

Hansberry, Lorraine. *A Raisin in the Sun.* New York: Random House, 1959.

Hoye, Jacob, ed. *Tupac: Resurrection.* New York: Atria Books, 2006.

Magoon, Kekla. *The Rock and the River.* New York: Alladin, 2009.

Scott, Cathy. *The Killing of Tupac Shakur.* Medford, NJ: Plexus Publishing, 2008.

Sirvaitis, Karen. *Barack Obama.* Minneapolis: Twenty-First Century Books, 2010.

Williams-Garcia, Rita. *One Crazy Summer.* New York: HarperCollins, 2010.

Websites

All Music

http://allmusic.com

This online resource allows viewers to look up musicians' biographies, discographies, and more. The site includes a profile of Tupac Shakur as well as a collection of album reviews.

Alternative Intervention Models (AIM)

http://www.hearteducation.org

This organization, founded by Leila Steinberg in 1998, provides programs that confront juvenile crime and drug use, as well as promote artistic expression.

The Huey P. Newton Foundation—The Original Black Panther Party

http://www.blackpanther.org

This website has information about the history of the Black Panther Party, including videos, virtual tours, and profiles of famous members.

Official Tupac Site

http://www.2paclegacy.com

Tupac's official site includes Tupac's quotes, photos, news, and more.

Tupac Amaru Shakur Foundation

http://www.tasf.org

The official home page of Tupac's foundation includes news about upcoming events, information about performing arts camps, a photo gallery, and more.

Tupac Shakur Media

http://www.youtube.com/user/TupacShakurRecords

The official Tupac YouTube channel features music videos, interview clips, and the *Tupac: Resurrection* documentary.

Vibe

http://www.vibe.com

Vibe magazine's website lets visitors check out hip-hop news, interviews, and videos.

INDEX

PHOTO ACKNOWLEDGMENTS

The images in this book are used with the permission of: © Al Pereira/ Michael Ochs Archives/Getty Images, pp. 1, 28; © Ron Galella/WireImage/ Getty Images, pp. 3, 50; © S. Granitz/Wireimage/Getty Images, p. 4; AP Photo/ Frank Weise, p. 5; AP Photo/Lennox McLendon, p. 6; Medio Images/Photodisc/ Getty Images, 8, 15, 24, 47 (top), 49, 59 (top), 68, 74 (top), 77 (top), 85, 89 (top); R. Marsh Starks/Las Vegas Sun, p. 7; © Librado Romero/The New York Times/Redux, p. 9; MTV Films/Amaru Entertainment/Paramount Pictures/ The Kobal Collection, pp. 12, 27, 89 (bottom), 95; © Bettmann/CORBIS, p. 16; © Business Wire/Getty Images, p. 17; Library of Congress (LC-USZ62-113271), p. 18; Seth Poppel Yearbook Photos., p. 19; © Peter Freed/USA TODAY, pp. 20, 65; © USA TODAY, pp. 25, 69; © Jack Gruber/USA TODAY, p. 22; courtesy of Leila Steinberg-www.alternativeinterventionprojects.org, p. 26; © Everett Collection, p. 29; © Warner Brothers/ courtesy Everett Collection, p. 31; © Pat Johnson/Retna Ltd., pp. 32, 34, 36; © Neal Preston/CORBIS, p. 35; © aerialarchives/Alamy, p. 37; Island World/The Kobal Collection, p. 38; Peter Brooker/Rex Features USA, p. 39; ©Lawrence Schwartzwald/Sygma/ CORBIS, p. 41; © Jonathan Alcorn/ZUMA Press, p. 43; © J. Vespa/WireImage/ Getty Images, p. 45; © COLUMBIA TRI STAR /ZUMA Press, p. 46; Columbia/ The Kobal Collection/Reed, Eli, p. 47; Columbia/The Kobal Collection, p. 48; © Henryk T. Kaiser/ Monsoon/Photolibrary/CORBIS, p. 51; Kimberly Butler/ Time & Life Pictures/Getty Images, pp. 52, 80; AP Photo/ Justine Sutcliffe, p. 53; EG/Globe Photos, Inc., p. 54; ERIK PENDZICH/Rex Features USA, p. 56; Krussberg/Photoreporters/Globe Photos, Inc., p. 57; © Krusberg/ Hulton Archive/Getty Images, p. 59 (bottom); © Chris Cozzone/Zuma Press/ Newscom, p. 61; AP Photo/Lauren Greenfeild/VII, p. 66; © Gobi, p. 70; Orion/ The Kobal Collection/Watson Glenn, p. 71; © Kelly Jordan/Globe Photos, Inc., p. 72; © Malcolm Payne/Time & Life Pictures/Getty Images, p. 73; © Berliner Studio/ BEImages/Rex Features USA, p. 75; © Ethan Miller/Getty Images, p. 76; Everett Collection /Rex Features USA, p. 77 (bottom); © Chris Farina/CORBIS, p. 78; AP Photo/Ron Edmonds, p. 81; © Imagno/Getty Images, p. 82; © Scott Gries/Getty Images, p. 83; Polygram/The Kobal Collection, p. 86; © Graham Whitby-Boot/Alistar/Globe Photos, Inc., p. 87; © Keith Winter/Getty Images, p. 88; © Robb D. Cohen/Retna Ltd., p. 90; c. Foxsearch/Everett/Rex Features USA, p. 91; © Henry S. Dziekan III/Getty Images, p. 93; Paramount/Everett/RexUSA. com, p. 96; WENN/Newscom, p. 97; © Robb D. Cohen/Retna Ltd., p. 98.

Front cover: © Dorothy Low/Contour By Getty Images; back cover: © Ron Galella/WireImage/Getty Images.

ABOUT THE AUTHOR

Carrie Golus has been a freelance writer since 1991. She has written hundreds of magazine and newspaper articles, as well as website content, brochures, video scripts, press releases, and the text for a museum exhibition. She holds a BA and an MA in English language and literature from the University of Chicago. Her titles include *Jim Thorpe* and *Muhammad Ali* for the Sports Heroes and Legends series.